The
Slinky in My
Coffee!

Tidbits of Memory in Roughly Chronological Order

By

Sue Brems

Sue Brems

Formatted, Converted, and Distributed by eBookIt.com
http://www.eBookIt.com

ISBN-13: 978-1-4566-3898-6 (hardcover)
ISBN-13: 978-1-4566-3897-9 (paperback)

DEDICATION

This book is dedicated to my brother, Cleon Robert Nixon III

+++++++++++++++++++++++++

The title is my brother's, and there actually was a Slinky in his coffee. One evening, my younger sister was playing with a Slinky toy while the five of us talked over our after-dinner coffee. My brother asked to 'see it for a minute,' and when Beth handed it to him it spronged off her hand and plopped into his coffee mug.

Since a Slinky stretches when pulled by the end coils, and since the coffee was hot, it took some time for Bobby to fish it out of his cup. Beth was worried about her plaything rusting. Mom, Dad, and I were helpless with laughter, and Bobby, gingerly pulling at an ever-longer stretch of metal, announced he had the perfect title for the book. "When I write one," he said, "I'm going to call it There's a Slinky in my Coffee. It's as catchy as Please Don't Eat the Daisies, and it's true"

SO, BOB, THIS BOOK'S FOR YOU.

Someone lifts me up to the broad sill of a
BIG window and stands in back of me so I
won't fall. Behind me is a dark room with
other people in it. I don't know who they are!
Outside, there isn't much light either.
I look <u>way</u> down and see lots of umbrellas - all
black, and shiny with rain. From the left, along
the grey street come marching men and moving
vehicles - a horse and wagon, square black cars.
That's all I see.

This image was so persistent that I finally asked Mom and Dad if they could explain it. For some time, they were at a loss too.

What they finally came up with was that I was remembering President Franklin Delano Roosevelt's funeral procession in 1945 – two months after I turned three.

Uncle Allen was an attorney and worked for the Interstate Commerce Commission. His office building was on Constitution Avenue, the route FDR's casket took from Union Station to the White House when it came back from Warm Springs GA.

Since Uncle Allen's office faced the street, he invited friends and family members up to view the cortege in comfort. Why I was brought along neither Mom nor Dad knew. Perhaps there was no one to look after me, or perhaps Mom and Dad thought it was part of history and that I should be there. Whatever the reason for my presence, I am glad I remember it.

HOWEVER SHADOWY, THIS IS MY EARLIEST MEMORY

CONTENTS

SETTING THE SCENE

Before there was a Beltway, we lived in the Greater Washington Area, which consisted of the District of Columbia and its Maryland and Virginia suburbs. The US Capitol was, and still is, the focal point of the city, with avenues named after states radiating from it like wheel spokes from their hub. The three that were important for us were Connecticut, Wisconsin, and Georgia Avenues.

The house I grew up in was three blocks east of Connecticut; the elementary school was three blocks west; and Leland Junior High School was southwest of that. Bethesda-Chevy Chase High School, on the other hand, was farther west, just off Wisconsin Avenue – so close, in fact, that when my friends and I were seniors, we could leave the school grounds for lunch, walk up there to the White Castle for sliders, and make it back to class in 45 minutes.

The other spoke in our life wheel was Georgia Avenue where our church, Calvary Lutheran, was located. Before I went to high school, I was completely unaware of the Wisconsin spoke because we spent so much time at church and in driving to and fro. Even during the relatively sleepy '50's, the trip was almost half an hour each way.

We were aware of other Avenues because they were mentioned now and then: Pennsylvania Avenue, of course, because the President lived there; Florida Avenue because it had a dangerous neighborhood we weren't supposed to go into; and Rhode Island Avenue for some reason that I can't remember. Still, our world consisted of the sector between

Georgia on the east and Wisconsin to the west, and those arteries took us wherever we needed to go.

This gave us a kind of cozy feeling—limited, but not restricted. Venturing into unknown, unrecognizable territory was easier because we knew we only had to find one of these avenues to lead us back home. As far as my brother and I knew, there were no reputations or stigmas attached to areas; they were merely directional identities.

Unfortunately, the ring roads of the Interstate Highway System have changed that perception. "Inside the Beltway" has become synonymous with out-of-touch attitudes toward the 'real world', while people who live there are considered condescending, intellectual to a fault, and rigid in beliefs.

Chevy Chase, which now is located inside the notorious beltway, had no such reputation before the 1970's when the ring road was completed. It was happy to be a link between DC and the rest of Maryland, but was a proud, self-contained, and peaceful entity, and it is still so. The nineties' speculation in real estate resulted in several beautiful old houses being bought and torn down to make room for McMansions, but my former neighborhood banded together and refused to sell any more property to developers, preserving what they all termed "our dignity." The Chevy Chase Women's Club Hall—that venue for the awkward 7th Grade cotillions—was where my 50th high school reunion held its welcome party in 2009.

IT LOOKED VERY MUCH THE SAME!

HOW IT BEGAN

T he saying "Luck has nothing to do with it" doesn't apply to me because luck has everything to do with who I am and what I've become. In fact, the older I grow, the luckier I feel.

I was born during World War II, but it started long before that, and it is thanks to The Great Depression and FDR that I am here at all.

My mother grew up in Racine, Wisconsin—at that time populated by first- and- second generation immigrants, mostly German. The population consisted of farmers and small businessmen, few with higher than an eighth-grade education, but with skills that helped the town to prosper and grow. My mother and her siblings were 'townies' because my grandfather owned a dairy, and the family lived next to it. The family included, besides my mother and grandmother, an older brother Paul, a younger brother Frederick, and an adopted cousin whose mother died of tuberculosis. Her name was Myra, and she and Mom were born in the same year (1913). People used to mistake them for twins.

"Are you sisters?" people would ask.

"Yes," was always the answer.

"Are you twins?" many asked.

"No," they always replied.

"My, my, what is the age difference, then?" the curious would ask.

"Three months," they would answer. They would then walk away and never explain.

Everyone in the family, which included my grandfather's eight brothers and their broods, attended the German Lutheran Church. Mom and her siblings attended the attached school that took students through the eighth grade. Many stopped school at that point, but Mom and her sister and brothers completed high school. Mom even managed to go to Carthage College for a semester, but the Depression interrupted her studies, and she left school to help out at home.

At first, she worked in the Dairy's office and later at various local businesses. The Dairy went under, and her salary was almost the only income for the household. Putting her hopes aside, she resigned herself to the Racine lifestyle – which for women was usually "kirche, kuche, und kinder."[1] She once told me that she expected to be fat by the time she was forty like her aunts and her mother.

Dad, on the other hand, had the big city childhood that Mom probably longed for. After his parents' divorce, he, his younger brother Bill, and my grandmother moved back to Washington DC from Osage OK where my Grandfather Nixon had moved early in its statehood. The three of them returned to 4001 Harrison Street in northwest DC—home to the Peacock family, of which Grandma Natalie was the second of four daughters.

Dad's childhood was usual for a city boy. School, family, and excursions to local government buildings where some of his relatives worked. His grandfather had served in the Spanish American War with Teddy Roosevelt, and Dad might have been steered in a military direction except that he had a

---

1 Kuche = kitchen; Kirche = church; Kinder = children

serious illness as a teen. It left him with a weak hip and a slight limp. He finished school just as the Great Depression began to spread. Having no prospects of a job, he returned to Tulsa OK for a time. While he was there, a new government program called Social Security began. The headquarters were to be in Baltimore MD and would need hundreds of office workers as it started up. The government set hiring quotas for each state to ensure equal participation in the scarce job market. Because Dad had established residence at his father's, he took the Civil Service exam in Oklahoma.

After some discussion with the family and some strong objections from her father, Mom traveled to Milwaukee to take the test. After a long wait they both received notice that they were hired. My Mom and Dad met working in the Social Security Administration Building in Baltimore. It was 1938; they were both in their mid-twenties. They were married June 11, 1940, in a garden wedding at 4001 Harrison Street. None of Mom's family was able to attend, so courtly, old Grandfather Peacock gave her away. I was born in John's Hopkins University Hospital, Baltimore MD on February 26, 1942, two months after the US declared war on Japan.

If Dad had still been living in Washington DC, he might not have been selected for the SS job, given the number of applicants in that area. So, thank you Social Security and President Roosevelt for bringing them together and allowing me to grow up in our fascinating nation's capital.

C. R. NIXON JR. AND MARIE KRENZKE –
ENGAGEMENT PICTURE

SILVER SPRING TO CHEVY CHASE

My world completely changed in 1945, and I have very hazy memories of life before that.

World War II ended. Europe's VE Day was May 8th. VJ Day on August 14 brought the Pacific War to a close. I was three and a half.

A month later, I had a baby brother named Bobby, and in December we moved from Silver Spring to 6505 Fulton Street in Chevy Chase. I had my own bedroom that overlooked the big oak tree in the front yard, and another window opposite the bedroom window of someone who would become forever associated with my childhood. This is the only house I remember.

I grew up in it, came back to it during university holidays, and was married from it in 1963. The family moved shortly thereafter to a different house in the same area, but I have always been grateful that they let me 'age in place.'

The Nixon family of four fit into the house and the neighborhood very well. There was a small bedroom that was Bobby's for nine months of the year – until Grandma Hattie, Mom's mother, came for her annual three-month visit. We were crowded then, but Grandma baked bread which made up for the inconvenience.

Bobby moved in with me during those times until we got too old to share a room. By that time, though, we had refinished the basement. It was a pine-paneled wonder of a rec room with a sofa and a bed, and a seat built around the steel support pillar in the middle of the space, portions of which lifted up for storage. Bobby or I moved down there when Grandma came so we all had our privacy. In fact, Bobby moved down there permanently when he started high school. His friends liked to come over and play poker, at which time no family member was allowed to enter.

The piano sat in the living room next to the front door. Mom tried to keep the top clear, but the temptation to put whatever we were carrying on top of it as we entered was an unfortunate habit she never succeeded in breaking. When the stack got too high, she would clear the pile, sort the things according to owner, and leave them inconveniently on our favorite chairs or our places at the dinner table so that we would have to put them away.

We also had a fireplace in the living room where we hung our stockings at Christmas and a door leading to a side porch that we sat on in the summer after supper. Air conditioning was not a standard feature in homes during that time, and DC summers were hot and humid. A breath of air before going up to hot bedrooms was a must. Later, Mom and Dad had the porch screened, and this became our evening gathering spot for reading or talking.

The dining room had a bay window that always held our Christmas tree. Around the middle of December, Mom would clean and dust this space, polish the small-paned windows, and decorate them with glass wax to look like snowflakes and piles of snow. Coming home from school and seeing the window looking wintery like that made us feel really Christmassy. When the tree went up, Mom made sure to turn on the lights before we got home so that the whole window sparkled at us as we approached.

The kitchen wasn't big enough to seat four people, so even breakfasts were eaten in the dining room. We each had a place at the table, and we sat there even if we ate alone. Dinner was the only meal we routinely ate together, and this took place every night. We were expected to be home on time. We always prayed the "Come Lord Jesus" grace together, and we were supposed to stay seated until everyone had finished. If the phone rang, Mom or Dad would answer it, say that we were eating, and return to the meal.

NOTHING WAS SUPPOSED TO INTERRUPT FAMILY TIME.

THE FULTON STREET HOUSE

GOING TO JAPAN

D ad went to Tokyo in the summer of 1949. He had been working at the Pentagon for the Army Air Corps since about 1943, and he was chosen to be part of a budget team needed to support the occupation of Japan. Bobby and I were told that we would go later – when our port call came, so I spent the summer waiting for the telephone to ring. It rang a lot, but it was never from "port."

In July we moved in with Aunt Ruth and Uncle Allen because our house had been rented for the two years we were supposed to be gone. Their house was nice, but it was on a busy street, and our play was limited to the quiet, shadowy rooms and the backyard that didn't have a proper swing. After the safety of Fulton Street's dead end and the kid population for playmates, this was a comedown. They owned a television, though, so we were introduced to Howdy Doody, Buffalo Bob and Clarabelle the Clown, and the program became the highlight of our day.

By late August, it was obvious to Mom that we weren't going very soon, and I suppose she felt we were imposing, although I am sure Aunt Ruth didn't make her feel that way. So, much to our relief, we moved again – this time to Racine, WI, where Mom grew up. We rented a large apartment in a grand old house, called the Stoeffel House, that had been split into two flats, and Grandma Hattie came to share it with us. The upstairs flat was occupied by a Catholic family with three boys, who were only sometime playmates since the youngest was slightly older than I. Two of them were Tommy and

Jack, and it was from Jack, I think, that I received my first non-proposal of marriage.

"I like you," Jack declared, "but I can't marry you. It would be a mortal sin."

There were other firsts. We went to see Mom's Uncle Henry and Aunt Marie on their small dairy farm between Racine and Milwaukee. I got to help collect eggs and watch milking, and I finally found out where milk came from. I had always wondered how the milkman could make all that milk he delivered daily. Being city kids, Bobby and I had seen only pictures – nursery rhyme ones at that – of farm animals. It was a real revelation for me, especially accompanied by the smells.

My grandfather had lots of siblings who still lived around the area, and we were soon confused by all the aunts, uncles, and cousins who turned up everywhere. There was also Aunt Myra who worked in a fascinating beauty shop and had a little magnet to attract hair and bobby pins that dropped on the floor. She let me do this when I visited her, and I started making plans to become a beautician. She cut my hair also – the first time I had had it done professionally. I wore a cape and everything!

School began, and I attended St. John's Elementary, Mom's former school. It was attached to St. John's Lutheran Church, and in the best clustering tradition, was right next door to the Catholic church and school. A chain link fence separated the playgrounds, and the older boys on either side threw stones at each other during recess. I was registered for second grade, but because I could read the word 'grocery' in the title of a favorite book, I was skipped to third grade where I had Mom's former teacher, Miss Krug.

I kept up with the class in all subjects except arithmetic. Second grade, which I had bypassed, apparently taught children to add and subtract, so third grade had many oral drills during which problems were called out and pupils competed to answer correctly. I could never win whatever reward was bestowed – a chance to erase the blackboard, say, or (my favorite), the ability to take an extra book from the school library -- so I memorized all the possible combinations and was at least in the running. This helped my self-esteem, but it did nothing for my knowledge of arithmetic. Later, in algebra, when letters took the place of numbers, I was lost and had to repeat Algebra I in summer school.

The school had no lunch program, so I went home for lunch. The Stoeffel House was two blocks away from school on the same side of the street. I had only to cross two side streets— the one next to the school and the one near our apartment. A teacher saw me safely across the first one, and Mom or Grandma waited for me on the other side of the second. I felt so grown up being able to walk those two blocks on my own. There was a candy store on the corner opposite the school, and if I begged enough, I returned home at 3 with a treat for Bobby and me.

One afternoon, we students came back from lunch to find the assistant pastor sitting at Miss Krug's desk. He waited until we were all seated and then said, "Remember our Bible lesson from this morning about heaven? That is where Miss Krug has gone." He then explained that she had eaten lunch and was having a cup of tea when she died. We were all very sad, and some girls cried with their heads down on their desks. I hadn't known Miss Krug long, but I felt sad enough to do the same although I wasn't sobbing like they were. It just seemed like the thing to do. This was my first experience with the death of someone I knew. To me, it was solemn, but not frightening because of the gentleness of the deceased and the gentle way we were told.

The Stoeffel House was endlessly fascinating because of the high ceilings, dark woodwork, and small cubbyhole spaces. The enclosed back entry was dusky, with a small window that looked onto an alley. From there I could watch coal being delivered to our basement. A long chute protruded from the coal truck and went through the basement window. Coal rattled along the chute and into an area in the cellar next to the furnace. I am not sure who stoked the furnace—probably Jack's father.

The kitchen had a real ice box with a drip pan. Several times during our stay, the iceman would come through the outside door into the back entry with a block of ice in enormous black tongs. He would open a small wooden door on the kitchen wall and slide the ice block into the refrigerator compartment, and we could keep food cool for another four weeks or so. During this time, we took turns emptying the drip pan on the floor beneath the ice box. I was only allowed to do this when it had little in it because it was wide and flat and unstable.

The house was a perfect Christmas house. It looked like all the houses in the classic children's Christmas stories, so we weren't really disappointed when we had to stay there for the holiday. There was so much family to celebrate with, so many goodies to taste, so much snow to make atmosphere, that I don't remember missing Daddy at all. Mom made prune kuchen for breakfast, and this became a tradition, followed even after all of us married. There was also kringle – a flaky dough with the most delicious fillings.

Mom and Grandma worked hard to make a merry time for us. Mom made a wardrobe of doll clothes for my doll Marianne, all by hand since she had no sewing machine. Marianne traveled in real style. She had a flower sprigged black skirt and a pink blouse, a blue sateen suit with a white collar, a corduroy coat and tam, and a sundress and bonnet out of yellow, red, and brown cotton. Gram crocheted accessories like purses and hats and capes, and she gave me Mom's old doll with a china head that I immediately named Rose because of her bright cheeks.

I don't remember what Brother Bobby got that year except for a book called "Bobby Had a Nickel" that began:

> Bobby had a nickel
>
> All his very own.
>
> Should he buy some candy,
>
> Or an ice cream cone?

We read this book over and over, along with the Babar books, and could recite the text along with Mom, but I can't recall what Bobby finally did with his money.

Of all the gifts under that tree, though, the smallest and, perhaps, the least expensive made the biggest hit and became the longest-lasting story game our family ever played.

A little package revealed a family group of jointed plastic dolls, about four inches high. They could stand while propped, sit in doll house chairs, and reach out their arms. Bobby and I immediately called the taller ones Mother and Father, and we wanted the children's names to match the initials M and F. Mary was an obvious choice for the girl, but we had trouble thinking of one for the boy.

Throughout the day we asked the relatives and friends who dropped in, but no suggestion seemed quite right. We finally got around to asking Grandma Hattie:

"Do you know any boy's name beginning with F?"

Until later, we didn't understand why she laughed.

"Why Frederick, of course," she said.

Only later did Mom explain that our grandfather and her younger brother (our uncle) were called Frederick and that the Krenzke family had had Fredericks for generations. That Christmas, however, we didn't know and didn't care where the name came from. The boy was christened Frederick, and the era of 'Mary and Frederick' (as in, "Let's play Mary and Frederick") began.

MARY AND FREDERICK

The Mary and Frederick family (it never had a last name) set up housekeeping in a bright blue leatherette train case with a strap handle on top. It was sparsely furnished at first, but the four of them soon acquired an array of plastic and wooden household goods from dime stores, toy stores, and people's attics.

Most elegant was an oval dining table with four matching chairs; most intriguing was the bureau with drawers that opened. There was a fuzzy green sofa, a dressing table and mirror, a set of miniature tableware in a cardboard "silver" chest, and an assortment of lamps, dishes, and even an ironing board.

I remember getting a baby crib with a side that went up and down, but there was no baby to sleep in it. M & F families seemed to materialize fully grown. So, Bobby and I began saving the babies that came in Cracker Jack boxes. In time, we had so many that they would not all fit in the crib even if we lined them up sideways.

The family grew in other ways also. Aunt Pearl (in a white dress) was Mother's sister. So was Aunt Ruby in bright pink (there's a theme here). Cousin Charlotte, looking very much like Mary, came along later. Her parentage was uncertain – sometimes she was Aunt Pearl's daughter – sometimes Aunt Ruby's. An unnamed uncle appeared from somewhere and stayed around until he became Father after the 'accident.'

The adventures of this family paralleled the Nixons' travels, so the first trip we took together was to Japan. Somehow,

Father lost his legs while crossing the Pacific, turned into an invalid, and also became much smaller than most of the family. He was quite easy to misplace, so Unnamed Uncle stood in for him when we had only a short time to act out our stories. On a car trip after we introduced our little sister Beth to the game, she accidentally dropped legless Father out of a window somewhere on a highway in Indiana. We wanted to go back and look for him, but Dad refused, so we decided that he had died because of his legs and that he was much better off in heaven where God had probably supplied him with a new pair. Unnamed Uncle took Father's place permanently, and the game continued for years.

The family even went to school with me one time. That was when the sixth-grade class was studying the movement westward, and each of us was assigned a 'project'. Since we were reading the Laura books for the third or fourth time at home, Bobby and I (and Beth if she didn't touch) were sending Mary and Frederick west also. I narrated the preparations and packed the covered wagon with household goods described in detail. Bobby would wait a certain amount of time and then, when I took a breath, would say "MEANWHILE, Father and Frederick were out by the woodpile..." or some such manly location. He then took his turn at narration.

We constructed a covered wagon out of a kitchen match box, with pipe cleaners curved across it to hold up the handkerchief that was the wagon cover. The wheels were made of cardboard and fastened to the matchbox with pins. They didn't turn, so we had to slide the wagon full of people and furniture across a table or bare floor. They fought Indians and forded creeks and met with dire snowstorms (*The Long Winter*) and arrived unscathed at destinations we only had seen on a map.

When the sixth-grade project was assigned, I was all set. I commandeered a shoebox and decorated it to look like prairie. I set it up as a background to our Mary and Frederick wagon, placed them in it, and told the story of their westward trek. I think I got a good grade, but that really didn't matter. The rest of the class were fascinated with M and F, asked lots of questions, and looked at me with envy.

FOR A TEN-YEAR-OLD, THAT WAS HEADY STUFF.

FATHER, MOTHER AND FREDERICK AT HOME

PASSPORT PHOTOGRAPH, 1950

ON THE WAY

T he trip across the Pacific began on a train. Port had finally called. We were to leave in March – from Seattle, Washington, and getting to the west coast from Wisconsin involved three days in a Pullman car from Chicago.

We had a four-seat section with two couches facing each other and a tip-down table between them. Bobby and I played Mary and Frederick endlessly on this surface. M and F found it hard to stand up though, and they had trouble keeping their house straight too. Their furniture kept sliding on the curves and at every clickety clack, someone fell over.

When we tired of setting things to rights for them, Bobby and I repacked the little blue suitcase – our most important piece of hand luggage – and listened to Mom read stories. We weren't allowed in the aisles unless Mom was with us, so we never ran through the cars like some of the other children on that train.

We really didn't mind this restriction. It was quite an adventure to go to the bathroom three seats away and an even bigger one to go to dinner in the dining car because that involved negotiating the gangway connection between cars. These flexible corridors jiggled. They were cold. The floor was metal, and the pieces didn't move in sync. Stepping from one side to another was frightening, and we needed Mom's steady hand to even attempt it. I got the hang of it after a few tries, but Bobby, being much shorter, never got over his fear.

Because we were such obedient children, the conductor granted us permission to "take a look at the observation car" at the end of the train. Mom and another wife and we children went to the glass-domed carriage while we were traveling through the Rocky Mountains, and the scenery was impressive. We were all enjoying the views when the conductor appeared and told us we had to leave. "I said you could take a look at it," he explained. "But I didn't mean you could stay. This is only for first-class passengers." No one else was there, but he insisted that we leave anyway. That was the only flaw on the Seattle portion of the trip.

What Bobby and I liked best was the nighttime transformation of the Pullman into a sleeping car. At a certain hour, the porters made berths out of the seats and created cozy little cubbyholes by hanging green curtains from the edges. Each upper cubby had a window that slid open so we could lie and watch the scenery. It also had a light so we could read or play until we were sleepy, and it had a ladder to help us climb to the upper berth, or down to Mom's if we got lonesome. Bobby and I were supposed to sleep head to toe in the upper, but Bobby usually slept with Mom down below. Once I woke up while it was still dark. The slide was open so I could see lights in the distant landscape; but when I peeked into the car itself, I saw a long, dark, spooky corridor shadowed with swaying curtains. I lay down again and made up stories until I fell back to sleep.

My memories of Seattle, Bremerton WA, and the port where we boarded the USS Morton are all in black and white. I think these come from all the photos we took, so I recall that time as pictures, not experiences. The only standout feelings from that brief visit were of an elegant Auntie Irenn, a tall and balding Uncle Paul whom I could not picture as Mom's brother, a small boy named Michael, and a sneaky and bratty girl named Michelle – our cousins, Mom said. Michelle was always playing tricks and then denying that she had done anything, and I didn't like her at all.

I remember a big hall where we checked in – I suppose they checked passports, travel orders and visas there. It was full of noise as hundreds of women and children tried to wait patiently through the hours that it took to be processed. The mothers might have been patient, but the children certainly weren't, and the shouts and crying and laughter echoed off the walls and ceiling of what was probably a hanger of some sort. Mom said once that having Uncle Paul with her shortened our wait simply because he was a man among all the females. He kept his temper and talked reasonably with officials. He knew his way around the area, and he knew which officials could expedite our check-in.

I liked Uncle Paul, but that was the only time I saw him. I'm sure the grownups kept in touch, but I never had an urge to write to Michelle, so, except for birthday cards from the family and a piece of driftwood art as a wedding present – created by Aunt Irenn – I lost all contact.

ON THE OCEAN

The Ship I Sailed On

U. S. Naval Ship General C. G. Morton

In 1950, after service in the Pacific during World War II, the USS Morton became a transport ship carrying repositioned soldiers to new locations and delivering dependents to their spouses at occupying bases throughout the area. It was our means of travel to get to Daddy in Japan. My memory of the ship is cloudy although I can see the lo-o-ong, narrow corridor leading to our cabin (201 on E Deck, according to Mom's trip diary) and a shadowy room with four bunks and a round window that looked like the front of a Bendix washing machine. I know we ate in the dining room and went to movies in the lounge (because of the same diary), but I can't recall any of those places.

I vividly remember only two things about the voyage. I got seasick on a chair. And I sang a public solo for the first and last time.

We sailed from Seattle WA on March 17,1950, at 3:30 PM, heading first to Alaska to leave troops at a base and then to Yokohama – the nearest port to Tokyo where Daddy was. At first, we could hardly tell we were moving unless we went outside and watched the shore getting smaller and smaller. The next morning however, we were in open sea, and Bobby and I awoke to find the chairs in our cabin sliding back and forth across the floor as the ship rocked. There were no grownups in sight, so of course we scrambled down from our upper bunks to take a ride.

Bobby and I sat with our arms locked around the backs of our chairs and skittered all over the cabin bumping into the wash basin and the bunk posts and sometimes the door. It was wild. We were having a marvelous time. When Mom returned from wherever she had been, she stopped the fun by making us get off and get dressed for breakfast. When I tried to stand up, I couldn't and felt so dizzy and sick that I had to go back to bed. The ship continued to rock, and my head seemed always to be rocking the opposite way. I remember staying in bed most of the day. It didn't matter, though, because a steward came in while the others were at breakfast and tied the chairs to a bedpost. No more rides – not that I cared.

Mom read "The Wind in the Willows" to us, and we played Mary and Frederick a little, but the winter sea was rough, and it took a while to get our sea legs. When I felt better, I went to the children's activities in the lounge and enjoyed them, I think. I don't remember not wanting to go. Every day was pretty much the same, and the time passed slowly. Each day the clocks were set back one hour. One Friday night we went to bed and woke up on Sunday morning. Bobby and I couldn't figure out why this happened. Why skip Saturday – the best day of the week?! It wasn't until much later that we realized we had crossed the International Date Line – the imaginary time marker line in the Pacific that matched the Prime Meridian running through Greenwich, England.

We were due to dock in Yokohama on March 31st, so there were many festivities on the last two or three days. The one involving the children was a party and 'talent' show where we kids were encouraged to perform. Bobby and I had learned a repetitious song called "Froggy Went A-Courtin'" that had seemingly endless verses about Froggy and Miss Mousie and their wedding, accompanied by also endless "M-hms." We were supposed to sing a duet at the party/show, but at the last minute Bobby wouldn't do it.

Mom notes in the diary that I got a prize for singing it myself, but I don't remember that part of it. All I remember clearly is standing in front of a bunch of people I didn't know and seeing Bobby on Mom's lap, where I wanted to be too. I guess I sang it all right. I am sure I didn't sing all sixteen verses. I don't even remember any applause. All I wanted was to get back to obscurity. For a long time after that, I avoided any activity that required a solo performance.

We docked at 2 PM on the 31st and saw Daddy on the shore, but he didn't come and get us for a long time, it seemed. I don't remember what he gave Bobby as a welcome present, but I got a Japanese doll that I still have. She is dressed in a red kimono and has short black hair. The photos of us that day picture four happy people, glad to be back together. We didn't realize then how much the next two years would influence all our lives.

THAT ADVENTURE WAS STILL AHEAD.

SUSIE WITH DOLL FROM DADDY, YOKOHAMA – 1950

JAPAN INTRODUCTION

When I flew to England from continental Europe in 2001, I left from Hahn Airport-75 miles from Frankfurt, Germany. The taxi ride from the city center was long, expensive, and deposited me in a bucolic area that seemed unsuited to such a modern purpose.

I was flying out early the next morning, so I stayed overnight at a long, low motel – the only accommodations in the vicinity – which was situated in a settlement of sorts close to the area's main road. The surroundings looked like a golf course with walking paths between low mounds of green, but they were dotted with large grey cinderblock buildings, all of them empty. I felt slightly uneasy.

I walked the half mile to a pizza restaurant – again, the only place to eat anywhere near – feeling as if I were in a movie dream sequence. You know the one: the character strides in slow motion, feet obscured by mist, toward something beyond our sight. As I walked, I saw more of the gray buildings bearing giant, faded numbers on their sides---86, 123, 97 they shouted.

I began to think the airport had been built on the grounds of a former prison, but why was I feeling prickles of recognition? Why did I think I had been here before? Our first trip to Europe had brought us nowhere near this part of Germany, so close to the then East German border.

It was a Twilight Zone moment. I even heard the music in my head.

While I ate the terrible pizza (no place in Europe, including Italy, can beat Papa John's thin crust) I contemplated finding another place to spend the night, but there was nowhere else around. As I walked back, the sun was setting, and everything was eerily quiet. I wasn't even sure that I wanted to **sleep** in this place, but I really had no choice.

Suddenly I saw a smaller grey building that I hadn't noticed before. It was also built of cinderblock, but it had wide steps and double doors and a faint lettering above this that announced that this was an ELEMENTARY SCHOOL. In English! In Germany!

The eeriness dissipated and a rush of nostalgia took its place. I was on a former United States Air Force base, built for troops and their families who were stationed there during the Cold War. The efficient U. S. Armed Forces uses identical plans to create bases for occupying troops no matter where they are deployed. Forty years before, I had walked similar routes on the base in Japan – to school, to the chapel, to the Px to buy candy bars. Now I realized that my motel had been the office which always sat just inside the compound entrance gates to issue passes and check IDs. I knew this place. I <u>had</u> been here before.

I SLEPT WELL THAT NIGHT.

JAPAN

T here was no such thing as culture shock in 1950. It was called adjusting then, and it was something we were supposed to do, so we did it.

Nothing could have been more different from suburban Maryland than post-war Tokyo. The recovery from the 1945 firebombing attack was not complete. There were some raw, new buildings – mostly official-looking ones; a few – like the Takashimaya Department Store – were still in progress. Yet, my memory is of rutted dirt roads, shells of buildings, and heaps of rubble, while my impressions are full of noise and smells. Ox carts with their 'honey buckets' were numerous, and there seemed to be no order to the traffic. Pedestrians walked in the road, and car horns created right of way.

Shopping on the now-glittering Ginza was like walking down the midway of a county fair with small booths on either side selling toys and used clothing and household necessities. Dinners were often cooked streetside because most living quarters had no ventilation for the smoke from hibachis that used charcoal for fuel.

The Black Market thrived. Bobby and I frequently recognized things we had seen in stores at home and begged Mom and Dad to buy whatever it was; but, as government personnel, they were not supposed to contribute to this illegal commerce. We wouldn't have understood any explanation, so they must have had a job shutting us up!

Grant Heights, the base we first lived on, was in Tokyo's northwest region, and it was built near a former kamikaze airfield. It doesn't look so far from the city on current maps and probably doesn't take very long to drive there now. But for Bobby and me, relegated to the back seat of a staff car, the trip seemed endless. Hardly any roads were paved either, which made for a bumpy, tummy-unsettling ride.

Once past the MPs at the gate, however, we reentered the US. No thatched roofs or shoji (sliding paper and wood doors) here! Recognizable houses, paved streets, signs in letters – these all gave us a feeling of peace and quiet and order that we hadn't felt since we left Seattle.

And – it was absolutely uniform. Official buildings were grey concrete, and the houses all were a cream stucco with green trim like the color you see on copper when it oxidizes. Homes were arranged in groupings called courts which were horseshoe-shaped sections with a grassy space in the middle, outlined by a path. I remember the houses being connected, but they weren't in long rows. Instead, four-home units were placed evenly around the court. Each family had a helpful name plate fastened to one of the porch pillars just in case you forgot which was yours.

Each house also had a full-time maid assigned to it. Our maid's name was Teruko, and we thought she was the prettiest of them all. Many were live-in maids, but Teruko couldn't stay overnight because she had to care for her mother, so later we got a houseboy too. Mac (Takeshi Hashimoto) went to school during the day and slept in a small room off the kitchen at night. He was almost like an older brother, and he was our babysitter when Mom and Dad went out.

TWO ENGLISH STUDENTS, MAC, TERUKO AND MOM, 1950

Within two weeks of arrival, I started school in Grant
Heights. I have no recollection of the school or the teacher or
any schoolmates. I don't know if I walked there or rode a
bus. I can't remember any lessons I learned in that third-
grade class. All I remember is wanting to be home with Mom
the way lucky Bobby was. He had a friend, too. His name was
Johnny Rounds, and he lived in our court. The two boys were
the same age (although Johnny was bigger) and they played
together every day while I was stuck in school.

Even though I didn't have a particular friend on that base, I
was once invited to spend the night with someone in the next
court. Despite the uniformity, each court had a different feel,
and each house had a unique atmosphere, even though
identical furniture was provided for the quarters. As soon as
I walked into that girl's house, I knew I wanted to go home. I

don't remember what I did or how it came about, but the girl I was visiting ended up spending the night with me.,

In retrospect, this was probably my response to a culture shock that wasn't supposed to exist. In the past nine months I had lived in three different houses, left two sets of friends behind, and crossed both a continent and an ocean. I hadn't adjusted yet, not even to having Daddy back. The only constant in all this had been Mom, and I wanted her nearby – like in the room, or, at the farthest, downstairs.

The only other sharp memory I have of Grant Heights is the monsoon season. This arrived just as playing outdoors began to beckon. It rained – and rained – and rained. We didn't care if the growing rice needed the water. Bobby and I wanted to play outside. The front porch wouldn't do; there wasn't enough of it anyway.

So, we must have been annoying enough that Mom gave up and let us out. There is a picture of the pair of us standing in the middle of the court looking wet and bedraggled, with water nearly to our knees. Very soon we were ready to retreat. Mom was right, a lesson had been learned, and things were back to normal.

PLAYING OUTSIDE DURING THE MONSOON, 1950

ADJUSTMENT ACCOMPLISHED!

WASHINGTON HEIGHTS

J ust after the Korean War began, we moved to an Air Force base nearer the city.

Washington Heights brought us closer to the chaos and smells that had so appalled us just five months before, but after living at the edge of rice fields, we welcomed the excitement. There was so much to do, both on base and off.

"Can we get lost today, Mommy?" was Bobby's question when he wanted to take a ride in our new car. We had acquired a Ford Prefect from a journalist who was being sent to another foreign assignment, and once Mom mastered the left-hand shift and the right-hand steering wheel, we went exploring. Getting to know the outskirts of Tokyo usually meant losing our way, and finding the way back was part of the adventure.

Asking someone was not much help because English wasn't widely spoken, and the accents of those who did were almost unintelligible. Because following these questionable directions usually got us more lost, we discovered lots of little tea shops and roadside markets and met some helpful natives who were truly kind to their foreign occupiers.

The Japanese address system was a major part of the problem. Buildings on a street were numbered in the order they were built, regardless of location, so Number 5 might be next to Number 21. Added to that, many houses had been destroyed so that the system seemed even more random when some numbers didn't even exist.

The only way to find a specific house was to use landmarks. Clusters of trees, hills, crossroads, heaps of stones – all these were used to give directions.

AND THEN THERE WAS THE FALLEN LAMPPOST!

In our directions to an American missionary's house one day, we were told to turn left at the fallen lamppost. These missionaries had been in the area for several years, and no one had cleared away this ruin, so they felt confident giving us these instructions.

When we got to what we thought was the spot, however, we saw no fallen lamppost, or fallen anything. Up and down the rutted street we drove looking for left turns and lampposts in every possible weedy patch. Finally, we spied a rare sight in rural Japan – a sign in English saying, "THE FALLEN LAMPPOST WAS HERE." Just the day before this get-together, the landmark had been removed, and because our friends didn't have a telephone, there was no other way to let the guests know.

It served the purpose that afternoon and far into the future because fallen lampposts came up for years – every time we had to give anyone directions to anywhere.

Pastor Danker, head of the mission, got Mom and Dad involved in non-military expatriate life very quickly. As soon as we began attending the Tuesday evening services, Mom and Dad were recruited to teach Bible classes, English classes, and Sunday School classes for both children and adults. Dad's teaching was usually done in the evenings and on weekends, but Mom's could be any time. I often came home from school to find our living room filled with young students from Tokyo University or women wanting to improve their English and their job prospects.

A number of these students made efforts to keep in touch with their "sensei's" (or respected teachers), and we heard from them throughout the years after we returned to Maryland. Several of them became prominent in business and government, and, in official capacities, visited the US. If it was possible – and they went to great lengths to make it so – they made side trips to visit us, bringing, as always, gifts for the "honorable Mr. and Mrs. Nixon."

Through the church, we also found Lutheran military families, and many actually lived on base with us, so Mom and Dad's social life picked up considerably. Evenings were devoted to canasta parties, or several couples would go off-base for sukiyaki or for dancing at the Komachi Inn. Bobby also found friends in this group, but as the oldest child, I often ended up "playing" with a bunch of four- and five-year-olds at these get-togethers. I liked it best when the adults went out because the maids watched the kids then, and I had time to read.

My world expanded in other ways also. By the time school started, I had become a Girl Scout, and I began attending meetings that were held in the Post chapel. I attended Sunday School there too, mostly because my friends did. I went to the Lutheran services on Tuesdays, so Mom and Dad didn't mind my getting other religious input – as long as I knew where I belonged! My friend Mary Charlotte was a Girl Scout too. She lived in the same court as I did, and we played dolls most afternoons. Sometimes we swapped them for a day or two, but that meant that we had to pack up their clothes, which was a LOT of trouble, so we didn't do this often. Marianne visited most. Rose always stayed with me.

When I started fourth grade at Yoyogi Elementary School, I could already greet people properly in Japanese (Ohayo – like Ohio) – for 'good morning' and Konnichiwa and Konbawa (for 'good afternoon' and 'good evening' respectively) – and I thought I was pretty good. However, I found that there was much more to learn. I can still count to ten, even after seventy years, because we recited "ichi, ni, san, shi, go, roku – with a rolled 'r' – shichi, hachi, ku, juu" over and over. (I remembered the last three in particular because I thought they sounded like a sneeze). We learned a song to the tune of "London Bridge is Falling Down" that taught us more phrases, and we sang this for a Japanese fourth grade class on one of our exchange days.

I sat next to a boy named Michael. Together we rode bikes all around the camp, and he was bold enough to go outside the gate on the Meiji Shrine side of the post despite the MPs telling him not to. I thought he was very brave because they had guns and stuff, but he daringly rode out on the path to the shrine, making a wide turn before coming back. I sent him an anonymous Valentine, signing my name with a 19 and a 14, which stood for my initials, but he guessed right away so the secret was out. I don't remember if he gave me one. After discovering that numbers could represent letters, Mary Charlotte and I corresponded in code for about three months.

Bobby, too, had school. He was five and was enrolled in kindergarten. Mom took him to Yoyogi on the first day, planning to pick him up for lunch. About mid-morning Bobby arrived home, surprising both Teruko and Mom. At recess he either decided that school was over or that he didn't really want to be there, so he just left and went home. The miracle was that he remembered the route and found the right house given the similarity of post architecture and layout. After Mom explained that he had to stay, he endured school for the rest of the year, but I believe he felt it was a waste of time.

Sung to the tune of "London Bridge is Falling Down"

Ano ne, Ano ne.	*You know what, you know what*
Mushi, mushi ano ne	*Speaking, speaking you know what*
Aso desuka.	*Oh, that's how it is.*
Chotto mate ku da sai	*Wait a minute if you please*
Ku da sai, ku da sai	*If you please, if you please*
Chotto matte ku da sai	*Wait a minute if you please*
Aso desuka	*Oh, that's how it is*

I truly don't know how the Japanese children felt about this cultural appropriation.

THE FORD PREFECT, OUR FIRST CAR. BOBBY IS IN THE FRONT PASSENGER SEAT.

HOLIDAYS

K ids think of holidays in categories. There are holidays when you have to go somewhere – like church – and holidays when you don't – like school. For some holidays you give gifts, for some holidays you get them, and sometimes there are holidays when you do both. Some are during cold weather when you can't be outside, and some come in hot weather when you can have a picnic on a blanket. Holidays are national, and religious, and personal.

We still had our usual ones in Japan, but we also celebrated some different kinds of festivals. Japan had festivals called Girls' and Boys' Days on March 3 and May 5, respectively. Girls' Day didn't seem to have much fun in it. The Japanese girls dressed in their best kimonos and went to the shrines. They got little presents and played with an arrangement of dolls in their homes. It was kind of a boring celebration as far as I was concerned.

Boys' Day was much showier and more active. Families who had boys would proudly hang paper carp banners outside their houses to show how many sons they had. I always wondered why they didn't fly something for their girls also. Weren't they proud of the girls, too? On that day all the boys got to play with balls and racquets and had special things to eat. It was a much more exciting day and very unfair, I thought. I mean, Daddy hung up a fish for Bobby!

Another celebration was cherry blossom viewing. Children weren't involved with this one. As far as I could tell, grown-ups would go out and sit in a garden and look at trees. The trees were pretty with rosy blossoms, but I wondered why you would have to sit there so long; they all looked alike! Mom and Dad were invited to a viewing party at someone's house, and it was an honor to be included, I think, because Japanese people didn't (and still don't) entertain at home much. So, they went and were gone all afternoon.

New Year was a big holiday. The US has one night and one day to welcome the new year; Japan had at least four days, and the whole country seemed to shut down. No shops open. Nobody working, not even Teruko or Mac. Houses with what looked like leftover Christmas tree branches on the outside. New year was never like that in Chevy Chase!

We had our Christmas, almost the same as at home. Daddy was finally with us, and we had friends on the base and in the missionary community to celebrate with. Two families who went to the Lutheran English services on Tuesdays were military, and one lived in Washington Heights, so we saw them that day. They had a little baby named Timmy, and I got to hold him, which was very special. The other family came from another base for the afternoon, so we had lots of people around.

My big present was a bride dress for Marianne. Mom had borrowed a sewing machine and made it from some white satin and lace. Mary Charlotte's doll got a bride dress too, and we met to compare the outfits. At first, I was disappointed because Mary Charlotte's doll had a much longer veil, but when I looked at the dresses, I was satisfied because mine was much prettier, I thought. Rose wasn't left out either. Teruko had made a kimono for Rose out of pink material. The dolls are long gone, but I still have both costumes. They were made with such love I couldn't throw them away!

CHRISTMAS IN WASHINGTON HEIGHTS, 1950. L TO R: RONNIE, SUSIE HOLDING TIMMY, GB, AND BOBBY.

BRIDE DRESSES FOR CHRISTMAS

Other events weren't holidays, but they were memorable. I remember the dedication of the Lutheran Center in the middle of Tokyo. It was on a weekend day, maybe a Sunday, and involved Sunday School and a church service, just like at home. The Sunday School class consisted of the missionaries' children, Bobby and me, and some Japanese youngsters. The building was still so new that there weren't many chairs or other furnishings. Our class sat on boards that rested on wooden boxes, and we sang "This Little Gospel Light of Mine" with gestures. Only the grownups had chairs during the service. And the head missionary's daughter, Beth, and I spent the night with the Sunday School teacher! And I didn't even want to go home!!

I only recall one trip that lasted longer than an overnight which we could call a holiday. We had to get permission to travel more than 50 miles from Tokyo, and Daddy had to get leave to do so, which is probably why we didn't go on vacation very often, or for very long. This time we went to Kyoto and Lake Biwa, which are roughly 300 miles south and west of Tokyo, and on the way, we saw Mt. Fuji! It looked just like the pictures.

Kyoto was a surprise because it was the first city we had seen that hadn't been bombed. There we saw a five-level pagoda (representing Earth, Fire, Water, Wind, and Heaven, we learned); we saw lengths of silk being washed in the clear water of canals; we fed the tame deer in Nara Park; and we saw people working contentedly at their jobs, who bowed to us as we passed. What we didn't see were shells of buildings, heaps of stone, or rutted roads.

We stayed for three days at the Biwako Hotel overlooking the lake. It was a hotel requisitioned by the occupation forces for troop rest and recreation, so it had western food, dining tables more than twelve inches off the floor, and the Stars and Stripes flying proudly on the flagpole outside the main entrance. We had a huge corner room on an upper floor which had high, wide windows on both outer walls. Bobby and I could sit on one of the beds and look out at the lake and the flat fields of rice spread out below, and at the flapping flag that was almost on a level with our eyes.

During dinner one night, there was a sudden hustle and bustle. Waiters whisked dishes from tables as soon as they were emptied, windows were closed in the dining room and hall, people scurried around carrying wooden shutters, and we were encouraged to finish quickly and vacate the lower level. Typhoon Kesia was about to hit the area, bringing wind and rain as it crossed this narrow isthmus to the Sea of Japan.

As we were climbing the steps, the wind struck the hotel, and we could see hotel personnel, leaning against the glass front doors to keep them from blowing off while water swept in underneath them. In our room we saw a panorama of the storm: wind and rain swirled in different directions at once, carrying unidentifiable objects with it; the rice plants bent to horizontal; the flag's rope strained away from the pole. No one had had time to lower the flag, so it whipped back and forth. It got darker and darker and more and more frightening.

Bobby and I played Mary and Frederick (yes, they had come too) for a while, and Mom read to us, but no one could ignore the storm for long. It was too noisy. And after a while, we just sat and watched the flag which was holding on bravely to its pole. The rope never broke, but little by little our stars and stripes disappeared with the wind. The bottom strip went first; then the outer edge frayed; then another and another stripe tore away. Then the blue and white field with its forty-eight stars started to unravel, but by that time it was so dark that we could no longer see it well. I don't know how well Dad and Mom slept that night, but we children had a good long rest.

In the morning, the storm had blown out to sea. It was quiet and the sun was shining. The first thing we did was look at the pole. There, waving in the pleasant breeze, was a valiant strip of red and blue – still hanging on.

NEITHER OF US HAS EVER FORGOTTEN THAT NIGHT.

The other celebration I remember is a personal one. Since we attended church on Tuesdays, I could go to the Post chapel on Sundays with my friends. At the beginning of the year, the

Chaplain announced that the Revised Standard Version of the New Testament had been published in a new edition and that those who came to church every Sunday for a year could earn a copy of their own. I signed up immediately. I would never turn down a free book!

Unfortunately, Dad's foreign assignment was finished that summer, and he chose not to re-up, so we were to go home in July or August. I was distressed and went immediately to the Chaplain to tell him. He thought awhile. Then he said, "I will give you a Bible verse to memorize every day. I want you to come and recite it to me each day for the next two months. If you do that, you will have your Bible." I went faithfully, and I still have the copy of the New Testament inscribed:

"Presented 1 July, 1951- In recognition of the successful completion of all required Bible memory work. Washington Heights Chapel Sunday School, Tokyo, Japan"

It was signed by Chaplain Elwood L. Temple with an added note from Lawrence S. Ritchie who was the superintendent of the Sunday School, that said, "It has been a pleasure to know Suzanne and her family."

I WAS VERY PROUD.

****

We left from Yokohama at the end of July, sailing for San Francisco. There was a large crowd of friends there to see us off. Beth Danker, the missionary's daughter, and I each had one end of a streamer, which meant that we would always be friends. As we sailed away, the streamer broke, of course, and we both cried.

That was the end of our stay in Japan, but it wasn't the end of our contact with the country or our love for it. The two years there were the beginning of life-long interests, friendships and most probably career choices for us.

HOME AGAIN

W e might have left Japan, but Japan didn't leave us. In fact, we brought some of it home with us so we wouldn't forget the adventure that changed all our lives.

The ceramic Hakata dolls created a Japanese market on our living room mantle with the old lantern painter sitting cross-legged on one side and the ruddy fisherman offering his catch on the other. The sweet-faced lady in the middle sold apples to one or the other depending on Mom's mood when she dusted.

Wooden Kokeshi dolls' heads bobbled in various rooms. The green vase with The Lord's Prayer in Japanese lettering – a gift to Dad from his Bible class – held daffodils in the spring. On a shelf in the dining room arch stood the "Japanese Abe Lincoln" – an ivory carving of a man reading a book as he walked with a bundle of wood on his back. I guess every culture has such a legend of perseverance and hard work.

Japan was on the dining table also. As peacetime industry restarted, Noritake again began manufacturing fine china, and Mom and Dad had the opportunity to order a set of one of the first post-war patterns. It arrived just in time to be packed in our shipment home, so the first chance they had to see more than a teacup was on our table in Maryland. It was always the dining room china. We <u>never</u> ate from those dishes in the kitchen, and whenever we saw the table set with them, we knew we were celebrating something special.

We picked up chopsticks as easily as forks, replaced ketchup with soy sauce, and munched on a kind of seaweed pretzel called osembei. Even Corky, the canine Nixon, was enthusiastic about this snack and would wiggle and roll with excitement when he heard the pieces rattle in the can. And he didn't even go to Japan!

We wore Japan, too. Not the silk jackets with dragons embroidered on the back, or anything like that; we wore practical and everyday stuff like the cotton, blue and white kimonos called yukata that we used for bathrobes, and the straw zori – the original flip flops – which we wore as slippers.

We became language snobs as well. We didn't actually **tell** people they were wrong, but we made opportunities to say a word 'properly' when it was mispronounced. A pet peeve was the word "sukiyaki" which the Japanese pronounced with a sibilant "S" and then "kiyaki" making the word three syllables long, not four. Unaware Americans said "sookiyaki," and this bothered us. Once when I repeated it after Uncle Allen said it wrong, he corrected me and went to great pains to show me how it was spelled. A frown from Mom stopped me from arguing - that time.

At other times we showed off – answering the phone by saying "mushi-mushi" or, inviting people in with "Dozo." We even wore "geta" – which were wooden clogs – outside, hoping people would ask what they were, but for some reason, questions never came up. After a while, we didn't waste Japanese phrases on the untraveled. They became family language, part of our private vocabulary, and we still use it amongst ourselves.

While most of our neighbors were familiar with the transient lifestyle, none of them had been to the Orient, so they were only politely interested in our experiences. Our closest friends thus became those connected somehow to Japan. Dad became an active member of the Lutheran Laymen's League which sponsored a program called The Lutheran Hour. This broadcast was, and still is, heard around the world. Through this organization, we remained in touch with the missionaries we had met in Tokyo and had yearly reunions at some central site – usually a camp facility – when they were on home leave. We called ourselves the Lutheran Veterans of Japan (LVJ).

I recall these long weekends as ordeals – more trouble than they were worth. I mean, why pack up clothes and equipment and food, lug it all the way to Ohio (or somewhere), and spend most of the time there trying to get the stove to work? For Vacation! Also, I was still the oldest, so my job was to keep the younger children happy and out of the grownups' way. Some vacation! Still, I got to see Beth Danker sometimes; the streamer had broken in Yokohama, but not our correspondence. Also, many of my friends in Maryland went to summer camps, so at least I had a camp to talk about too. I just didn't have any skate key lariats to show for it.

Our other Japanese contacts were Mom's students, and they were actually Japanese. A notice on the drugstore bulletin board requesting "a teacher of English conversation" led Mom to a procession of Japanese embassy wives all needing one on one instruction.

Mrs. Ohata was the first. Her husband was the Ambassador's legal attaché, responsible for answering any questions about Japan's new constitution which had been adopted in 1947 and was still being amended. Her children were Tetsuo and June, and June was just Beth's age – perhaps three. I would often come home from school to find platinum-blond Beth and coal-black-haired June playing together while Mrs.

Ohata had her lesson. They looked like salt and pepper shakers!

Through Mrs. Ohata and, later, Mrs. Tokoro, wife of the agricultural attaché, Mom and Dad were invited to many embassy functions including the opening of the annual cherry blossom festival (seats in the VIP section) and a tea reception in honor of the new wife of the Crown Prince who was making her first international tour as Empress-in-Waiting. Mom reciprocated by inviting the ladies to things they would not ordinarily have access to such as neighborhood coffee klatches and home Christmas parties. At a party one evening at our house, I taught Mr. Tokoro to cha-cha!

The Japan connection lasted all the rest of our lives – sometimes only in our minds, but often in reality as we met others who had lived or visited there. One serendipitous meeting was at a get-acquainted function during my first week at Valparaiso University. At a freshman mixer, I bumped into a red-haired girl.

Her name tag read, 'Nancy Tewes, Japan.'

"Japan," I exclaimed. "I used to live in Japan!"

As we talked, we discovered that we were ships that passed in the night – literally. Her father was hired to be treasurer for the Lutheran Mission in Tokyo, starting in the fall of 1951. She was crossing the Pacific TO Japan as I was sailing home. She knew all the same people I knew, like Beth Danker and the pastors. She, too, had babysat all those little kids.

We were instant friends. She came with me to Maryland for Christmas that first year, and we later roomed together until she left school to get married. We stayed in touch throughout our lives, even though we were unable to attend each other's weddings or see each other much. The friendship ended with her death from breast cancer nearly forty years later.

My sister Beth has often said wistfully, "Do you realize that I am the only member of this family who has never been to Japan?" She never had an opportunity to live abroad, but Bobby and I, infected by the "wanderlust virus," spent years overseas and look upon these experiences as significant periods in our married lives. While Bob and Judy had no kids when they went to Tonga, my husband and I were able to give foreign life encounters to our sons in two different countries.

JAPAN'S INFLUENCE ON ALL OF US CONTINUES TO THIS DAY.

CORKY

orky was a medium-sized package of energy that joined our family soon after we returned from Japan. Bobby and Dad went to the pound one day and came back with him, and all of us except Mom welcomed him enthusiastically.

Mom had reluctantly agreed that we could get a dog. "But it's your responsibility," she declared. "I'm not feeding it, or bathing it, or walking it, and I don't want it in the way or on the furniture." We solemnly promised – at least Dad, Bobby and I promised; Beth was too little, so we promised for her.

I would hate to say that Corky was ugly. He wasn't really, but he wasn't exactly beautiful either. He was sort of scrawny with a wiry black and brown coat, an appealing face, and a pointed tail that curved up over his back legs and wagged continuously. I don't know why, or even if, we named him Corky. Since he was about a year old when we adopted him, he might have come with it. But Corky he was to the end of his days.

He obeyed the rules. He didn't jump on furniture; he shadowed us kids, especially Bobby, when we were at home; and he seemed to know that Mom wanted him out of the way and curled up in obscure places while we were at school. When the family went out together, he was left outside "to guard the house" as Dad always instructed him when we left. He would follow the car to the edge of the lawn to see us off and then trot back to the porch where he stationed himself with his paws drooping over the edge of the second step.

Neighbors told us that he never left our yard while we were gone, and he was always there to greet us with his waving corkscrew tail when we pulled back into the driveway.

I don't remember his being on a leash, although we must have used one sometimes. Mostly, he followed Bobby around, even going down the slide with him. He chased the balls thrown, allowed us to spray him with the hose, sat at the foot of the back steps, seeming to listen to us read aloud, and almost became the fourth sibling in the Nixon household. As far as we were concerned, anyway. Mom remained distant and slightly disapproving, even though she softened sometimes when she saw how he played with us.

Beth grew up with him. As far back as she could remember there was always a dog in the family, which probably prompted her to have at least one in her household when she became an adult. She now adopts Scottie rescue dogs and has had a grooming business as a sideline job for several years. She was undoubtedly in training for this when she gave Corky a peanut butter massage.

Now, I only heard reports of this incident because I was at school, but it has become part of Nixon lore – that is, a story told often and altered slightly each time – and is necessarily from one point of view (Mom's) since Beth remembers nothing. So, I will relate what I have heard over the years and acknowledge that others may have different versions.

Mom always had a project, and this week it was redecorating the kitchen. In preparation for wallpapering and repainting, she had emptied the cupboards and the food pantry, unplugged the appliances, and taken down the curtains. The kitchen was tiny, so all this paraphernalia was scattered on various surfaces in the dining room.

Beth was somewhere between two and three and still needed supervision, so Mom created a little play space in the kitchen doorway – probably blanket and pillows, a doll or two, and Corky to keep her company. Beth and Corky seemed settled and content, so Mom began to work, listening for any sound that might suggest trouble. She heard no alarming noises, so she finished two walls and turned to check on Beth.

At first, all seemed well. No one was in danger. But a closer look showed Corky stretched out blissfully on the blanket while Beth busily and lovingly spread peanut butter on his stomach and back. His paws were relaxed, his eyes were closed, and his head rested against her knee. How Beth got to the peanut butter is a mystery. How she knew to choose the jar with spreadable material is another. But in the kitchen doorway was a sticky-fingered toddler, an even stickier dog, and a very messy blanket.

Work stopped immediately. Corky's massage was followed by a bath, most likely in the laundry sink in the basement. He reveled in the attention and was calm and obedient throughout. Beth had one, too, in the tub upstairs. I don't know what happened to the blanket.

Mom did not finish the kitchen in one day after all. A clean Corky was put outside and Beth was watched constantly until naptime, after which we were home from school and could play with her. We had sandwiches for dinner, and Mom completed her project on the weekend.

There are two lessons in this:

SILENCE DOESN'T ALWAYS MEAN THINGS ARE OK.

and

NEVER MAKE A VOW THAT INCLUDES THE WORDS 'NEVER' AND 'DOG BATH' IN THE SAME SENTENCE.

CHEVY CHASE CHILDHOOD

"No offense, but I think you had a really weird childhood," my daughter-in-law remarked, and so it must seem to a Gen X-er. I can't recall why she made this statement; it was probably in response to my description of an activity unfamiliar to the 'TV Generation'—those children born in the 1960's who grew up with Sesame Street, Captain Kangaroo, and Schoolhouse Rock. My childhood was post-war, but pre-TV. We were also the generation that was post-food rationing, but pre-MacDonald's and post party-line, but pre-direct dial for long distance telephone calls.

Spam was meat; chicken had bones; fresh fruit was seasonal, and pizza was an exotic foreign food. Without the educational programs to teach us letters and give us information, we played with alphabet blocks and scratched our names in dirt. We read books; we listened to radio programs like the Lone Ranger, The Shadow, and (if we were "sick" and got to stay home from school), the afternoon soap operas like Stella Dallas, Backstage Wife, and Fibber McGhee and Molly. We didn't feel deprived or bored.

So, whether my childhood was weird or not is debatable, but it certainly was a happy one. I grew up on the narrow dead-end block of a short street in suburban Chevy Chase MD. Like most of our neighbors, my father worked for the US Government; and like all the women in the neighborhood, my mother did not have a job outside the home.

The houses were modest, two-story, brick or stucco. Siblings often shared bedrooms. We did not have a car—not at first. In 1945, when we moved in, peacetime production was just beginning, and it would be several years before we owned a vehicle. Four blocks away, on Connecticut Avenue, we could catch a bus to downtown Washington DC. The walk to the bus stop was an exciting excursion, past some grander houses and a lot of pretty gardens, and past one church with many doors. Early on, I liked to knock on all of them and was very surprised once when someone answered. Although she was a very nice lady, I never "knock-knock-knocked" on that Heaven's door again.

Excursions to downtown weren't necessary for entertainment, though, because we had plenty to do on our street. First off, it was full of kids. Next door to our house lived my best friend Kay and her older sister Sheila. On the other side were the three Carpenter children—Chris, Carol, and Craig who was nearer my younger brother's age. Next to Carpenters at the dead end of the street were the Brenners with four boys—David, Douglas, Michael, and Alan. David and Douglas were the "big boys" while Michael fit into the majority age group. At the corner of Taylor and Fulton Streets lived the Millards with another Michael and Benji, my brother's special friend. Bobby and Benji often played together in Benji's big back yard, but the rest of us took to the streets.

Because it had no outlet only people who lived on it drove down our block, so the entire area was our playground. We practiced tennis shots against the garage wall at the far end. Hide and seek scattered us all over the neighborhood, with home base being the telephone pole on the curb between our house and Carpenters'.

Summer brought bike riding, roller skating and sometimes baseball, organized by the big boys. The elm tree across from our house was first base, the manhole cover in the road was second, Kay's steps were third, and someone's jacket was home plate. We never broke a window, but we often lost a ball that rolled down the sewer. Even worse was when a ball was hit into the Cleveland's yard. This older couple had no children, at least none living with them, and they were very proud and protective of their lawn. To retrieve the ball was an act of courage because Mrs. C would always berate the kid unlucky enough to draw the short blade of grass. The 'lecture' included respecting other people's property and an account of the effort it took to maintain their immaculate yard. It usually stopped the game for at least five minutes.

Three blocks away was Doc's Drug Store. It was located in a line of neighborhood shops, including a Safeway Grocery, a barber and beauty shop, and a garage with a gas pump. I suppose it would be called a strip mall or shopping center now. But the word "mall" wasn't in our vocabulary then. Except for the shopping district in downtown Washington DC, we shopped at locally owned stores. The pharmacist, Doc Shapiro, lived nearby. His children were older, but we all went to the same neighborhood schools. Doc knew his clientele well; he greeted us by name in the store, asked about us on the streets and admonished us kids to be careful when we overstepped boundaries. Inside the store, that meant messing with the things on the counters and, most especially, spending too much time at the comic book rack. "If you want to read it, buy it," was his refrain.

Along the right-hand side of the store was a soda fountain. Chocolate milkshakes and sodas were my favorite drinks, but I didn't often have enough money for one of those <u>and</u> an Archie comic. Most of the time I ordered a coke which cost a nickel. For much of my childhood, coca cola was a mixed drink consisting of a squirt of coke syrup, a stream of charged water, and a scoop of ice, finished with an efficient stir by the soda jerk. Because of this procedure, cokes tasted different depending on who was behind the counter.

As I got older, the soda jerks became my contemporaries—a place where local boys (always boys) could get a summer and/or after-school job. I could ask them for more syrup, or charged water, and even—later on—for lemon, lime, or cherry flavoring. Doc's was one of the first stores to get air conditioning, so this job sure beat mowing lawns in August. (DC was not called Foggy Bottom for nothing!)

Another attraction on that Brookville Road corner was the bi-weekly bookmobile visit. I don't remember going to a library in Chevy Chase, but I remember eagerly awaiting the bookmobile. We children were allowed to check out four books at a time, and these never lasted me two weeks. I did a lot of rereading at this time and supplemented borrowed reading material with our own collection of children's books.

The librarian on the bookmobile introduced me to *"The Diary of Anne Frank"* when I was eleven—a book and a woman I have never forgotten. I have kept my own diaries sporadically since then, inspired by Anne's phenomenal recording of her short life.

One of our memorable neighborhood events was the 1953 <u>Fantastic Variety Show on Fulton Street.</u> This was the transitional summer between 6th grade in Rosemary Elementary School and the more-or-less grown-up world of 7th grade in Leland Junior High, and the last weeks of summer dragged more than usual. Kay came home from Girl Scout camp, our new school clothes were ready, and time hung heavy. In the best Micky Rooney/Judy Garland tradition we said, "Let's put on a play!"

A neighbor's son and his wife lived next door to us at that time. The Carpenters had moved, leaving a great hole in the younger social set, but Mrs. Thompson was a cordial addition to Fulton Street: she had a TV that she let us watch sometimes, she gave us treats, and she didn't scold if we ran on her grass. Her son studied at the University of Georgetown, and his wife was doing a degree in drama at Catholic University. Jean, hoping to be a teacher, gathered us older kids in the back yard and had us reading Shakespeare aloud. "Romeo and Juliet" with its duels and balcony scenes impressed us the most, so naturally we put both situations into our play.

Having spent previous summers with the Shoes books by Noel Streatfield and "The Swish of the Curtain" by Pamela Brown, I was the most "experienced" (or at least the most informed) about amateur theatrics, so I became producer of the show. We worked on our play for several days. A balcony scene required a high porch with a railing, and also a girl and a boy to play the parts of princess and prince.

The princess was easy—Kay said she wanted to be the princess, or she wouldn't be in it; for the prince's role, we recruited Eddie Lyerly who lived three blocks up the hill on Taylor Street – the Brenner boys having flatly refused to join this venture. I was the King who disapproved of Prince Eddie's courtship and also (by shedding my mother's evening cape) the villain who dueled (aha! You see how we worked that in?) for the Princess's hand.

The duel outcome was, naturally, happy for the Prince and Princess, but because the fight was not fatal, jailing the opponent and getting 'him' off the stage for the wedding was a problem. We solved this by means of an arrest by my 7-year-old brother Bobby, who was cast as the Guard and various extras. Unfortunately for the impact of the finale, Bobby got so involved with the duel scene that he ventured closer and closer to the action until he was standing practically stage center. At the call, "Guard, seize him!" he realized that he was in the wrong place and darted in the opposite direction, back around the corner of the house, to make his planned entrance.

Rightfully amused, the audience doubled up with laughter-embarrassing Bobby, distracting the performers, and spoiling the triumph and poignancy of the denouement. Chuckles were heard throughout the touching union of the Prince and Princess by her father the King, who went from villain to ruler by donning the cape again. During the bows, Bobby got the most applause!

The audience was more numerous than we had hoped. We expected our parents, of course – 6 people at least – and we hoped that Mrs. Thompson would come, but as we knocked on neighborhood doors to invite the people in our vicinity, we scarcely expected a double row of spectators. Mom, in fact, quietly lamented that we were working so hard, and she was afraid hardly anyone would show up. Since the highest porch with a railing was the Nixon porch, and since most of the costumes and props came from Nixon closets, she was quite aware of the effort put in.

However, it was the end of summer, and one by one, other kids returned from vacations and wanted to take part in the performance. We added a couple of songs, a recitation, a dance, and an announcer to the program so that everyone could be included. Jennifer Broughton, the announcer, supplied the highest-ranking audience member. Her father was the military attaché to the British Embassy, but he and his wife cheerfully joined the other parents, and all the Fulton Street neighbors (even the Clevelands) in bringing folding lawn chairs and sitting in the road in front of 6505.

The program went on so long that it began to get dark before the finale - The Star-Spangled Banner sung by all. Kay's father, Mr. Shore, solved this problem by backing his car from the driveway next door and shining the headlights on the lawn. "

IT WAS THE PERFECT FINISH TO THE PLAY – TO THE SUMMER – TO CHILDHOOD.

TELEVISION

C hildren of the '40s and early '50s had little access to television. There was no children's programming on weekdays except "Howdy Doody" just before dinner and a weekly "Captain Video" adventure in an early evening slot.

In fact, there was hardly any daytime TV at all. But as the industry grew, more and more time slots were filled, and more age groups were catered to. When I was in junior high school, I remember rushing home so that I could watch an hour of The Micky Mouse Club with Bobby and Annette and Darlene and Cubby. My favorite parts of the program were the dance numbers and the Spin and Marty segment. I think I had a crush on Tim Considine and probably Bobby as well.

The first show I remember watching was "Howdy Doody" at my Aunt Ruth's house. She and Uncle Allen had always been the first in the family to get up-to-date items—cars, appliances, furniture, and, of course, the very newest status symbol – a TV. In 1949, while we waited for our port call to Japan, we stayed with them for a time, so my brother and I were able to see these magic pictures that had only been available in movie theaters before. They weren't colored pictures like "Bambi," but they were happening right before our eyes. We were mesmerized, which is probably why we were allowed to stay in the 'grown-up room' by ourselves.

The three networks had test patterns that appeared if you tuned in before they were on air, and they remained stationary until the programming started. That was what happened on the local channel that aired the "Howdy Doody Show." It began at 5:30, and just before the show appeared, a clock hand would circle the logo second by second. My brother and I would sit, chins in hands, and count along – FIVE, FOUR, THREE, TWO, ONE! Then came the magic words, "Hey, Kids. What time is it?" We would shout along with the lucky ones sitting in the Peanut Gallery, "It's Howdy Doody time."

We got our own television – a second-hand one – when I was eleven years old, and my brother was seven. It must have been during late spring because Mom and Dad hid it behind the open front door until after dinner. When they excused us, they told us to close the door, and that is when we discovered the surprise. By this time, we had seen programs on other people's sets, so we were extremely excited to have a TV of our own. It was an enormous piece of furniture with a tiny screen and 'rabbit ears' on top. This was the antenna that brought the signal to the screen. We soon learned how to manipulate the ears so that the picture was clearer and were able to watch shows by ourselves.

The biggest TV event in our early years of ownership was the coronation of Queen Elizabeth II in June of 1953. We didn't realize at the time that it was the first time a coronation had been televised. All we knew was that we could see it live. During the spring, my sixth-grade class had acquired a new member – a girl from England who had a 'funny' accent. Most of the kids giggled when she talked, but I, having read English children's books since the age of eight, was fascinated. The fact that she lived near me gave me a chance to walk home with her and listen to her say words I had only read before. Her name was Jennifer Broughton (pronounced Brawton). She had a little sister named Vivian and a governess - a Governess! - named Frances.

When the coronation was discussed in school, she was able to explain something about it, although she didn't really know much more than anyone else. At least what she told us was said in the proper accent. On the way home that day, we talked about it some more because our family had planned to watch it that evening. She told me that she wouldn't be able to see it since they had no television. Her parents were to join her father's colleagues at the British Embassy for a 'watch party' but no children were included. Impulsively, I invited her, her sister, and her governess to come over and watch with us. They all accepted enthusiastically, and her mother was effusively delighted. I was proud of my hospitality until I got to within a block of home.

Then it hit me!

I hadn't asked my mother if it was all right!!

I dawdled along trying to make up ways to tell her what I had done and to compose speeches of apology to Jennifer, Vivian, Frances, and most of all, Mrs. Broughton who was a little formidable. However, when I confessed my transgression to Mom, she was actually pleased. In fact, she was so pleased that she began to make something for refreshments and sent me to the store to buy candy and nuts.

My brother, grandmother and I arranged chairs in front of the television and sat in each to see if we could see all right. We had moved the TV to the basement room because it was too light upstairs to see the screen clearly, but we had never watched anything down there before. Grandma found some nice china dishes to hold the candy and nuts, and she insisted on ironing the napkins.

THAT WAS THE FIRST PARTY I WAS EVER
RESPONSIBLE FOR.

SCHOOL

We always called it Rosemary, but officially we went to Chevy Chase Elementary School. I started morning Kindergarten in 1947 with pretty, red-haired Miss Armstrong and severe-looking Mrs. Matthews as teachers. There I met my second-oldest friend. His name was Johnny Bassett, and he could read too!

Our parents weren't supposed to teach us to read in those days, so I'm sure we were a problem to the teachers. It was okay to know the names of the letters, but we were supposed to use certain procedures to 'recognize' words, not sound them out. He and I didn't do it that way.

Johnny and I did all the pre-reading worksheets and let our tablemates copy them, which sort of defeated the purpose. I can still remember one with sailboats that had the names of colors printed underneath. I told everyone what crayons to use until Miss Armstrong came over and shushed me. Also, both Johnny and I had heard most of the stories the teachers read to us and gave away the endings. We were definitely a threat to the system.

For some reason that I don't know, I was chosen to be May Queen and preside over the school's spring festival. My duties were to walk down a flower-strewn path, sit in a decorated chair, and watch the other classes' performances. Mom made me a long dress of satin with lace over it. It was beautiful, and I felt queenly indeed. I wore a crown, too, but that presented a problem.

The crown was large and made of tinfoil-covered cardboard – very heavy with flowers and slightly too large. Since my wispy hair had absolutely no traction, the crown kept sliding around, and twice it fell off. I wasn't used to being waited upon, so I hopped up before the 'court' could act and jammed it back on my head. Mine was a democratic monarchy!

The performance hit of the afternoon was the tonette band from one of the fourth-grade classes. They wore little red capes and hats and played several songs recognizably. I really hoped I'd get into that teacher's class. Forget satin and lace: I wanted a red cape.

Johnny and I weren't in the same first grade – probably by design. I had Miss Cheezum, a tall, gray-haired lady who looked stern but was really very kind. My stand-out memory of first grade is when I told a big lie in Show and Tell and then had to retract it.

I never seemed to have anything to say that was as interesting as the other kids', so one day I got up and announced that I had a baby sister. There was great excitement. Everyone was exclaiming how lucky I was and asking her name, and Miss Cheezum congratulated me. I had the attention I had longed for, but I didn't realize that it would continue and that I would have to make up more lies to maintain the story. Every few days something came up. What was her name? (Barbara) How much did she weigh? (I don't know). Do you hold her? (Not yet) It went ON and ON!

Finally, a friend from the class came to see me and asked to see the baby. I tried to stop the question, but Mom heard and said the damning words, "What baby? We don't have a baby." I was scolded soundly and had to stand up at the next Show and Tell and admit that I had told a lie. I have never forgotten that moment, although I hope everyone else in the class has. I would also like to state that it wasn't really a lie, just a serendipitous prediction, because four years later I did have a baby sister - named Beth.

Talk about teaching moments, though! I still have trouble telling any untruth – even white lies out of politeness.

The following school years were spent in various corners of the globe, but I returned to Rosemary for fifth and sixth grades. I had caught up with Kay while I was away, and to my joy, Johnny Bassett had skipped a grade too and was in both of these classes. I was finally at school with my two best and oldest friends.

I remember these years as full of activity, both in and out of school. I was a member of the School Safety Patrol in both grades and proudly wore my khaki uniform to school the days we had our meetings. The added advantage of this membership was that patrol meetings were on the same day as the Girl Scouts' (to which I still belonged). The Safety Patrol required that the uniform be worn, while the Scouts did not, so I didn't have to wear that bilious green dress with buttons down the front, which I hated. The khaki skirt and blouse were snappy and military-looking and much more attractive, I thought.

In school, our work became more project-based, and class time involved more group planning sessions than lectures and paperwork. We made presentations on history and social studies subjects, discussed books in reading circles, and even planted a garden at the side of the playground that belonged to us 'big' kids. On that playground we also played dodgeball and softball, jumped rope and played hopscotch, ran races, and swung on the parallel bars. When bad weather kept us in at recess, we moved the desks to the edges of the room and square danced.

We took part in the May Day festivals too. The May Queen was out of my reach – I was too old! So was the red cape – I was too old! I was eligible, instead, to dance around the Maypole in a ruffly skirt, but the girls picked to do that were slender and dainty, and I was charitably called 'sturdy.' Instead of satin and lace, or even a skirt, I wore denim overalls and a checked shirt and did a choreographed walk around the dodgeball circle with a rake over my shoulder. I was not happy!

The worst thing about the festival was the outside practice. It was the season for the seventeen-year locusts, and they were dropping on us from trees and crawling on us when we sat on the ground. The boys chased us with them too, so we girls didn't enjoy this activity at all, even though we secretly hoped that certain guys would pester us.

Because 1952 was an election year, and because the campaigning was local news, we planned campaigns for our class elections. All of us learned about the national parties and conventions; then we held our own 'caucuses' and planned strategy and campaigned for our candidates. The journalists, Johnny, Jim O'Brien, and some other students, even published a class newspaper that circulated throughout the upper grades. It was mostly about sports and people's pets and various classes' projects, but we did have a period when class election news grabbed all the headlines.

We ate lunch in the cafeteria, which for us was just outside our classroom doors. We could smell the food and know what we were getting before we stood in line and saw it. Fish sticks were always an option on Fridays – probably the only time I enjoyed fish of any kind. Macaroni and cheese was my favorite meal, but I hated the peas that went with it. The best dessert was Dixie Cup ice cream with a movie star's picture on the lid. Licking off the ice cream gradually revealed the face. Sometimes they had Jell-O with a dollop of whipped cream. I did <u>not</u> consider that an adequate dessert. (Probably this is where my 'sturdiness' came from.)

Most often, I brought a sandwich from home and bought a small carton of milk (7 cents per carton) to go with it. We purchased a monthly card that was punched for each milk bought. It became dirty and dog-eared by the end; and if you lost or forgot it, you had to pay your 7 cents each day until the next month's card was for sale.

Bobby did not like any lunches at school. I wasn't aware of this at the time, but he says he went home each day for lunch. Our house was some distance from school and getting there required crossing Connecticut Avenue – a terribly busy street. He maintains that he ran all the way home and back which probably used up any calories from his meal. His physical fitness was always far above mine or anyone else's in the family!

The transfer to Leland Junior High School was a real jolt for me. By the time we left Rosemary, our group was close and cohesive. Leland was much bigger, with at least four other elementary schools sending their students there. Jim O'Brien was in my homeroom, but no one else from Rosemary was. The many strange faces kept changing with each class, as did the teachers.' It was hard to get to know anyone well, and I hardly saw anyone I knew.

Johnny didn't join us at Leland. He went instead to a private school called Sidwell Friends. We all missed him, but our circle was already broken up, so it didn't matter as much as it might have. He <u>did</u> return when we entered Bethesda-Chevy Chase High School three years later, so even though Jim O'Brien had moved to Pennsylvania before ninth grade ended, at least most of our group was in the same school for one final time.

KAY, JOHNNY, AND I FINISHED HIGH SCHOOL AND GRADUATED FROM B-CC TOGETHER IN 1959.

BETHESDA CHEVY CHASE HIGH SCHOOL

CHURCH

C hurch was not a choice. Sundays were reserved. Attendance was expected. Faith was assumed— Lutheran faith, of course, which was the only kind there was, really.

Church mornings began early with soft-boiled eggs, toast, and juice, prepared by Dad. Juice varied with the seasons; winter often brought heated tomato juice – a special treat. Carbs could be Grandma Hattie's homemade bread, or prune kuchen, or ordinary store-bought bread with butter and jelly. But we <u>always</u> had soft-boiled eggs! Sometimes they were presented in egg cups ala our English novels. Mostly, though, we had them (two each) in sauce dishes, and we cracked them down the middle with our knives. It was easy, then, to separate the cooked part from the uncooked if Dad had not boiled them enough. None of us liked the 'icky.'

By 8:30 or so we were on our way to Silver Spring where our church sat on a small hill overlooking busy Georgia Avenue. Before it grew to its present size, the small stone chapel looked lonely in the large expanse of land, but at least there was plenty of parking. A good thing, too, since few of the members were within walking distance. There we spent the morning in Sunday School or Bible class and, of course, the worship service. Most of us participated in it in one way or another. Mom sang in the choir; Bobby was an acolyte when he was old enough (girls didn't do that then); Dad ushered most of the time, whether he was on the schedule or not; I often sat with Grandma Hattie when I wasn't singing with Mom. It was definitely a family activity.

Attending church wasn't limited to our family, however. Every visitor, whether casual night spenders, good friends, or distant family members, was invited to church, and assent was almost taken for granted. I can't recall the number of neighbors who came to midnight services on Christmas Eve and Easter sunrise services at dawn. I can't count how many girlfriends we took to potluck dinners who ended up helping in the kitchen. Dad always invited people to join us, and he concentrated especially hard on his own family members who were casual churchgoers at best. His mother, Grandma Natalie, had become a Jehovah's Witness which worried him greatly, but she remained staunch.

One willing visitor was Henrietta Krenzke, our Grandma Hattie from Racine. She made her home with us off and on for over twenty years, staying several months at a time. Grandma became a distinct member of the Calvary congregation – not just "a guest of the Nixons." She was a personality in her own right and had her own circle of friends, even her own offering envelopes.

One of her friends was Mrs. Wessel, a forceful person with a rather formidable physique. As our congregation outgrew our little chapel, folding chairs were set up in the overflow area once used as a social room. The aisle went down the center and the chairs were placed from the walls outward, so when seated, it was difficult to change places or move from one area to another. One Sunday, Grandma sat down on a chair near the wall and prepared herself for worship. All the rest of us were involved in service duties, so she was alone.

This particular service was unusually crowded, and Mrs. Wessel was unusually late. When she spied the empty seat in Grandma's row, Mrs. W marched up the aisle and ordered Grandma H to "sit over there" pointing to the chair by the wall. "So, I sat," Grandma explained, while we ate Sunday dinner.

This insignificant and mundane incident became a family joke, lasting for years. Using the phrase as a preface to any order softened the demand element in it, for us at least. This became so ubiquitous, though, that we forgot that other people didn't understand the joke, and we began ordering friends and acquaintances to 'Sit over there" which caused misinterpretation on their parts and chagrin on ours. We only have to say it amongst ourselves to trigger snickers, and we often do this on purpose at inappropriate times. Family jokes should be used frequently!

Before we lived in Japan, someone picked us up and drove us to church. We were dependent on these friends and had to adapt to their schedules. But when we came back from the Orient, we brought a car with us! It was a tan Ford Prefect with right-hand drive and two small lighted arrows that pointed left or right when we wanted to turn either way. Bobby and I liked to take turns sitting in the front seat because it looked as if we were driving.

With our own transportation we were able to go and come on our own time, or, more specifically, Dad's time. In his usual enthusiastic way, he became involved with the Building Committee, the Church Council, the Financial Planning Group, the Men's Club, Bible study classes, and various worship duties like ushering and greeting. Almost the only church activities he was absent from were the Ladies' Guild and the choir.

Mom, Bobby, Beth, and I often lingered in the narthex and/or the car for an hour or more after the service while Dad counted offerings, turned out lights, put things away, and made sure all the doors were locked. I often felt that having our own car wasn't the advantage I thought it was.

Sundays weren't the only church days. As we grew, we children also had activities that required us to spend large chunks of time there. The most important from viewpoints other than our own was confirmation class, which was held for two hours on Saturday mornings during the school year. Confirmation at age fourteen was a rite that granted us adult status in church membership, and we had to be prepared. So, instead of sleeping late and lounging around until noon on Saturdays, we were hustled out of bed, fed, and transported to church by 9 o'clock – every Saturday – for two years. Faithful Dad drove us and waited, using the time to do property maintenance or accounting or some other church duty he had shouldered.

The 12-14-year-olds sequestered in the classroom formed social connections/friendships beyond Luther's Small Catechism and Biblical substantiation. These grew stronger with attendance at our Confirmation Camp held yearly just before Pentecost – the traditional day of confirmation in most liturgical churches. Both students and older teens went on this fellowship weekend, and the younger were introduced to the Walther League.

This organization of the Lutheran Church, Missouri Synod, was a social/service group formed to counteract other, more "worldly" ones that could tempt these new Lutherans. The League, at individual churches, sponsored similar activities to the Scouts and the school service clubs which had quasi-religious elements such as an opening prayer-a practice we were not supposed to take part in. I think it was also to ensure that romantic interests would gravitate in the 'right' direction. In the '50's, marriage between a Catholic and a Protestant was considered a mixed marriage, and – especially in Maryland which was settled by Catholics, for Catholics, and had a large population of Catholics – the Lutheran Church did not want its young adults to 'stray.'

The League actually did this pretty well. I remember picnics, swimming parties (after the polio scare ended), trips to Glen

Echo Amusement Park, and the camaraderie of working together at church functions – usually helping at congregation dinners or decorating for Christmas. Occasionally, all the area Lutheran churches' Walther League groups would arrange a special outing like a boat trip to Mt. Vernon or a play at the Carter Barron Amphitheater. We often met in a park on the 4th of July to watch fireworks together.

The most memorable times though, were the dance parties. At church, these were always square dances (ballroom dancing not allowed), but parties at someone's home were much livelier and had better food. Everyone brought their favorite and most recent 45rpm records to dance to. We learned new steps; we jitterbugged; we slow-danced and stole kisses in the midst of a crowd. These parties happened mostly on Friday evenings. On Saturday night we were supposed to come home early to be ready for church the next morning.

One romance caught attention, not just of the teen group, but of the entire congregation. Brother Bob began a short-lived relationship with a girl named Janet Kennedy. This would not have been momentous in itself, but this happened in 1960.

In that year Richard Nixon and John F. Kennedy ran against each other for US President. There was much angst and a lot of acrimonious discussion about a Catholic becoming president, so a tender bond between any Nixon and any Kennedy was news. The entire congregation watched this affair of the heart with interest and speculation, which probably led to it being short-lived. As the campaign waned, so did their affection for each other, and both moved on. So did the country.

All three of us were confirmed at Calvary in due time. The examination ritual where the congregation hears the confirmands explain what they have learned in their classes was different for Bobby and me. I and my fellows (I was the only girl) had an evening of recitation. We memorized most of *Luther's Small Catechism* and recited practically all of it – sometimes in concert and sometimes alone. Bobby's examination consisted of a personal essay on "What Jesus Means to Me," which he read to the congregation. The church members probably received a much better insight into his faith than mine. What Beth did, I don't remember.

Dad and Mom made church the center of our family and our lives. Their commitment gave us a basis for faith that none of us has lost, although we have each made it our own and not a carbon copy of childhood belief. The three of us went to Lutheran colleges and met mates of faith. We are active in our congregations and our communities. Our children have been raised with a church background. I think Dad would have liked a pastor or a deaconess or two in the family, but we all took up service in some form.

THE TRAINING AND EXAMPLE OF OUR PARENTS HAVE
CARRIED US THROUGH THE MANY YEARS SINCE.

GAMES, PUZZLES AND ACTIVITIES

W e lost Rhode Island first. Connecticut went next. New Jersey disappeared much later.

The wooden puzzle of all 48 states was a fixture on our toy shelf. I don't know when we got it or who gave it to us, but it seems as if there was never a time when we didn't have it. We played with it endlessly, putting the States together and dumping them out again, more to hear the pieces knock together than anything else because all our other puzzles were cardboard. Constantly putting the country back together like that sure taught us geography.

By 5th grade, we could look at a blank map of the continental US and name each state by its shape. We could even do that after 1959 because Alaska and Hawaii were ink outlines floating in the Pacific on our puzzle board. The compass inked at the top helped us learn directions also, although at first, I didn't understand how going west could get us to Japan which is in the Far East! This puzzle map, along with Mary and Frederick, is probably the oldest of our toys and played with nearly as often.

The only board game I recall playing with Bobby was 'Uncle Wiggly,' who was an elderly rabbit with a lame leg, which forced him to use a candy-striped cane. We read the stories first, and when the game came out, we enjoyed getting him from his burrow to Dr. Possum's house. All the characters from the stories – like Nurse Jane Fuzzy-Wuzzy and The Skeezicks - either helped or hindered his journey, and you could play it whether you could read or not. We didn't have many board games, not even the popular ones like Monopoly. I guess we weren't capitalists!

We kids did play Monopoly sometimes - at friends' houses - but I thought it was boring and tedious. The most exciting part for me was at the beginning when we got the money and chose our tokens. However, I <u>never</u> won, and I always seemed to end up being the thimble! One game could last for days; but even before the end we knew that whoever had Boardwalk and Park Place would beat us all. It was usually the banker.

Scrabble was a family game, and most weekends we got the board out and sat around the dining room table playing that cutthroat word game. One combative word was "*rex*" which used the valuable X and gave the lucky player from 8 to 24 points depending on the square where it was placed. REX was challenged (by non-family members, especially) and defended so often that the dictionary practically fell open at the page, and we all finally memorized the definition:

REX is "An animal, showing genetic recessive variation, in which the guard hairs are shorter than the undercoat, or entirely lacking."

We could recite this at any needed moment. In unison, even!

When we were pre-teens, Canasta was our card game of choice. The trouble with this was that you couldn't play it unless there were more than two people. I mean, you COULD, but it wasn't much fun because you knew early on what the other person had and was collecting. We played it mostly when Grandma Hattie was with us because, even if Mom was busy, the three of us could play until she had time. Old Maid and Go Fish were card games that came in packets of "Children's Games." They were fun when the neighbors visited but not with family. We had better things to do together.

We saved all our religious Christmas cards faithfully, and in the summer, when it was steamy hot, we retreated to the coolness of the basement and made Christmas books. These were a project of the Lutheran Women's Missionary League (LWML). Using pictures cut from the cards and pasted on the blank pages of the books, we told the Christmas story. We used Bible verses to label the pictures – sometimes cut from the cards and sometimes lettered by hand. The books were distributed to children's hospitals and senior living facilities and sometimes prisons. I always wanted to help give them out, especially in the prisons!

Often, our friends would come and help us make these books. I don't know if they did it out of altruism, friendship, or the need to keep cool, but we appreciated their help because Mom usually got half a dozen blank booklets to fill. We spent most of August underground with stacks of cards and bottles of rubber cement, creating our works of art. Eddie Lyerly made the best books. He had an artistic eye for color and appropriateness, and we all tried to copy his careful efforts.

During the cold months we emerged from the depths and turned to comfort food. Our favorites were fudge and an exciting new dish called Pizza. Believe it or not, pizza in the '50's was hardly known and rarely found. It certainly wasn't delivered!

I don't remember where we first tasted it, but all of us developed a craving for it. And it was hard to get. The only place we found that sold this pie of our dreams was a small bakery near church, but it wasn't open on Sundays, and it closed at some impossible hour like 4 pm. Obviously, this didn't help us, especially since our mouths started watering for it at about 8 pm on Sunday night.

Finally, Chef Boyardee listened to our taste buds and produced a "pizza kit" with a dough mix (just add water), a can of sauce to spread on the dough, and a bag of 'parmesan cheese' that looked a little like sawdust. But it worked! It also tasted pretty much like we remembered, and it resulted in a pie large enough to cut into six wedges – just enough for each of us, plus Grandma Hattie, to have a slice.

A Chef's kit was always kept in the pantry for winter Sundays. When homework was done, we kids took over the kitchen and made pizza for the whole family. After a while, we got creative and embellished the sauce with chopped onions, leftover breakfast bacon and sliced olives, just for variety. All of us then sat around the fireplace, just before bed, burning the roofs of our mouths with hot cheese and wishing the kit made more.

Fudge was our other edible tranquilizer. Around Christmas, we made it the way our First Lady, Mamie Eisenhower, made it – chocolate chips, marshmallows and hot milk beaten until it all melted together. At other seasons, we used the old-fashioned method – boiling the chocolate/sugar/milk mixture to the softball stage and then beating it until thick, but pourable.

This was a fine art that we didn't get right a lot of the time. For one thing, none of us knew what the softball stage looked like when we dropped a bit of the syrupy stuff into cold water. The other problem was that if you beat the mixture too long it didn't pour and hardened inside the pot. If you didn't beat it long enough, it was chocolate soup.

We ate a lot of fudge with spoons - or speared on ice picks because that was the only way to get it out of the pot. It would have been such a <u>shame</u> to waste it!! We didn't discover candy thermometers until much later. They sure would have helped!

One evening, when we were making both fudge and limericks, the inevitable happened. The fudge became hard much more quickly than expected. While we tried to get it into a flat pan, it solidified at the pot edge, looking like a chocolate waterfall. Mom and Bobby immediately produced a limerick:

There was a young girl who made fudge

That from the saucepan wouldn't budge.

She grunted and groaned,

And twice loudly moaned,

"Please budge this fool fudge with a nudge."

ORIGINAL MONOPOLY PIECES

The last line is still used frequently in the family, usually in frustration. Making fudge was what we did the last evening before I was married. By then, pizza had become ubiquitous, but we kept our family evening tradition alive with the sweet stuff – with a thermometer this time.

IT TURNED OUT PERFECTLY!

BOOKS

I never really <u>learned</u> to read, and yet, I can't remember a time when I couldn't. There must have been some lessons that accompanied our color-named Dick and Jane reading groups, but I don't recall any. By the time I got to first grade I was already reading fluently, but I don't know how I got there.

Maybe it was because my childhood was filled with books from an early age. My mother often told the story of a three-year-old Me "reading" *Peter Rabbit* to a four-year-old neighbor and turning the pages at exactly the right times. She had read the book to me so often that I had memorized the text and the accompanying page turnings.

I don't know if I was truly reading in that incident because I don't remember it, but it was surely the beginning of my fascination with words. These arrangements of letters that created pictures in my mind took me to other places, other worlds, and I wanted to keep on travelling.

My first adventures were with Babar and Celeste; Ratty, Moley, and Mr. Toad; Dr. Doolittle and the Pushmepullyou; and Saltina and Squeaker—the grocery mice. Later there were Freddy the Pig and his cohorts, Ben Franklin and Amos the Mouse who lived in his hat, and Felix the Cat in the Sunday funnies.

Imaginary worlds led me to other times and places. While living on an Air Force base in Japan, I discovered Laura Ingalls Wilder and followed her west over and over. At first our entire family gathered before bed for a few read-aloud chapters of whatever Little House book was available from the school library, and these were often out of sequence. Home again, two years later, I gradually acquired the entire series, so the Nixons again took the journey with the Ingalls – in order this time. *The Long Winter* was read aloud more than the others because it became the traditional book for when we were sick in bed. It made us feel so cozy when Mom read us to sleep.

On the ship coming home, I discovered the Shoes books by Noel Streatfield and entered, not only pre- and post-war England, but also the foreign world of theater. I became stage struck, and *The Swish of the Curtain* strengthened that interest. As simple as these stories were, they are responsible for a life-long interest in the performing arts, a bucket-list resolution to see all of Shakespeare's plays live, numerous volunteer opportunities, and a popular and effective teaching method.

Nancy Drew and her sister detectives were much maligned by librarians in the 1950's, but I, along with my friends, devoured the books, traded them, and gave them to each other as birthday gifts with "Dibs on borrowing it first" accompanying the "thank you's" and "goodbyes" at the end of the parties. While they were formula fiction, all very much the same, I was fascinated with the wording and actually added some new vocabulary. 'Chum' and 'roadster' became familiar, and I learned that what one had for 'luncheon' was the same as what one had for lunch.

The Five Little Peppers were my friends for a while, and later Jo March and her sisters took their places. Anne Frank inspired me to keep a diary. Janet Lambert's books about life on an army base occupied my early teens, as did Betty Cavanna's stories of young romance in the world of dog training. Anne of Green Gables lasted longer because she grew up in the books. I loved the first book, but my favorite was "*Anne of the Island*," the third book, where she goes to college and finally falls in love with Gilbert. I was disappointed in how he turned out, though. He was kind of pompous, I thought.

Somewhere in my teens I began exploring the universe. Along with Dad, Brother Bob, and TV's Captain Video, I entered outer space, which (until Sputnik) was very much a fantasy world.

JULES VERNE * ARTHUR C. CLARKE * ROBERT HEINLEIN * RAY BRADBURY

All of them led me into utopian and dystopian existences, some of which were as horrifying as Jane Eyre's gothic mansion. Narnia and Middle Earth offered escape. Bad things happened there, too, but somehow, they were gentler experiences.

Modern science fiction became too technical – too real -- for me. I liked to believe other worlds existed, but I didn't particularly want them proven. So, when science overtook fiction, I retreated into realistic fantasy. Even now, as an adult, I spend time with my childhood favorites, and I often go to Hogwarts when my current life becomes a little too Dursley-ish.

All these and other books led me to an English major at university and an addiction to reading. I carry reading material with me wherever I go, and my bedside table always holds, besides eye drops and Kleenex, at least one book to read before I sleep.

My philosophy, as one of my T-shirts says, is:

SO MANY BOOKS, SO LITTLE TIME

READING ALOUD

Mom was usually willing to read aloud to us. When we were small the sessions were for quiet times – before naps, or when it was too hot to play outside, or, occasionally, when we could persuade her to do it for no reason at all; but the most regular and satisfying times were just before bed.

In my memory, the bedtime reading ritual began when we were waiting to go to Japan in 1949. In both Aunt Ruth and Uncle Allen's house and in the flat in Racine we had story time just before going to sleep – what therapists call 'winding down' now. The Babar the Little Elephant books occupied many an evening, and *"Nellie's Silver Mine"* was a book for winter nights in Racine because it was set in cold Colorado. Since Grandma Hattie was born in Leadville, she could add some first-hand reminiscences to the story

Mom's reading style was just a shade off the matter of fact, but she never had trouble keeping our attention. The narration was smooth, the dialogue was expressive but not overly so, and her pronunciation was never distracting. In fact, the only mispronounced word we discovered was "slough" in the Ingalls Wilder books. Mom pronounced it to rhyme with 'tough.' When we found out that it should be 'sloo,' it was too late: Laura and Mary lived on the edge of the Big Sluff, and that was that!

She never condescended to us by the overly enthusiastic and breathless delivery that kindergarten teachers and early TV children's show hosts used to hold listeners' interest. In fact, we were so spoiled from listening to her pleasant and conversational tone that we dismissed the other style and always squirmed a little if forced to listen to it. It wasn't really "reading"!

Mom's diary of our voyage to Yokohama tells of reading *"The Wind in the Willows,"* and I vaguely remember reading sessions in our cabin and in the lounge. The lounge always attracted other children, though; Mom was welcoming, but I (and I think Bobby) didn't want anyone else to listen. This was OUR mother and OUR book, and they had no right to butt in! Still, the reading did calm these unruly kids down. The steward told Mom we were the best-behaved children on the ship. The others ran wild, and the other mothers seemed helpless to curb their behavior. I think Mom thought that she was doing something to give everyone a break.

The Ingalls Wilder books absorbed us during evenings in our quarters, first in Grant Heights and later in Washington Heights—two air force bases outside of Tokyo. The series was read randomly because of the demand for them at school. When we returned to Maryland, Laura returned with us, and bedtime reading continued on Fulton Street.

Because Beth was little, I listened to family reading well into my teens. We all enjoyed gathering at the end of the day, and there was always a clamor for "one more chapter – please" when Mom thought we should be in bed. One time the chapter ended with, "Pa blew out the lantern" and Dad reached up and turned out his lamp. Story time was over! Mary and Frederick benefited from these reading sessions too. Whatever we heard in the evening story we reenacted with our M & F family. They had many adventures in Mr. Toad's motorcar, had tea with Ratty and Moley, went up in a balloon with Babar and Celeste and spent hours in the Little Brown House with the Peppers.

As we grew up, we continued reading aloud, but with an adult twist. When I was in high school, the five of us absorbed a chapter a night of the vocabulary builder *"It Pays to Increase Your Word Power"* – a sort of multiple-choice test of a book with chapter themes on Latin prefixes, words for big objects, and strange verbs, all joined by a narrative that helped you remember the new terms. We learned unusual vocabulary, competed to get more answers right than each other, and found ways to use the words afterwards. It was amazing how many fit into everyday conversation if someone really tried. When I took the SATs, I had no problem with the verbal section!

Reading aloud wasn't the only reading done, of course. All of us read independently too. It took Bobby a while to get into the habit, but Mom, Dad, and I had at least one book going at all times.

For Dad it was mostly religious reading. Having been recently confirmed in the Lutheran church, he spent time reading the Bible and its commentaries; *"Here I Stand"* – a biography of Martin Luther; and some educational material on the Catechism. To get to the Pentagon for his job, he had to leave early, so he breakfasted alone with *"Portals of Prayer"* which was a daily devotional booklet containing a Bible verse, a thought on the verse, and a short prayer. We often found it at his place at the table when we came down later. He had a small stand for it, and that became part of his place setting. We never removed it unless we needed the room.

Mom was an eclectic reader. She read all the books Bobby and I read as well as biographies and novels. I remember *"The Big Fisherman"* and *"The Robe"* sitting on the coffee table at one time and another, along with *The Saturday Evening Post* and several newspapers. Mom and Dad read the newspapers together, every night, each in their own chairs with their own lamps, passing the sections back and forth. Since Mom had made dinner, it was the children's responsibility to clean up. As we began the kitchen work, Mom had her quiet time with Dad. All of us were content with that arrangement.

I would rather read than play outside, especially in the sultry summers, and even more so as I got older. Many books were so fascinating that I couldn't put them down, even at bedtime. My bedroom, just off the upstairs hall, had enough light to read by if the hall light was left on. I often continued reading until Mom and Dad came up to bed and turned it off. Of course, I had to pretend to be asleep, and that meant that I creased pages and sometimes tore them as I dived under the covers and covered up the book. Once, as I was intent on coloring the end pages of *"The Swish of the Curtain"* they came up unexpectedly, and when I quickly feigned sleep, I broke all the crayons I was using and made a mess of my sheets. I also mistook colors. One boy ended up with a purple shoe.

Graduating from teen series books to suitable adult novels happened fairly early. I think I was thirteen when I read Agatha Christie's *"And Then There Were None"* which was so startling that I read it over and over. It never ceased to thrill at the end. More Christie mysteries followed, and I moved on to gothic classics like *"Jane Eyre."*

I learned to read plays and visualize the action in my head from the descriptions of the sets and the blocking, which were included in most published scripts. I didn't enjoy Eugene O'Neil, who was the critic's darling at the time, but I did like Tennessee Williams and read almost all his dramas. English teachers dismissed Williams' plays like they did Austen's novels, as frivolous – not worth the time, not Literature with a capital L. I, however, disagreed, and I pointed out that I was at least not reading 'kiddie' lit, which they had to acknowledge. To this day, I distrust critics' and academics' opinions about what to read. I prefer to figure it out for myself, thank you very much!

Brother Bob and I continued the read-aloud tradition with our offspring, creating another generation of readers and parents who read to their own children. Bob and Judy often read aloud to each other also, with traditions like the Christmas chapter of "*The Wind in the Willows*" on December 24th and Keats' poem on St. Agnes Eve.

I got out of the habit when my children grew up and out but have rediscovered its pleasures, at least the listening part, from an online site called Audible. For the first time, I could finish "*The Call of the Wild,*" which I always stopped reading at about Chapter 3 when the dog started to be treated cruelly.

I HAVE FINALLY FOUND OUT WHAT HAPPENED TO BUCK!

THE DINNER TABLE

D inner was always at six, when Dad got home. Except on Sundays when it was at two - when we all got home. This was the meal that had dessert – not a snack like cookies or something, but a planned one like pie or strawberry shortcake – with coffee to follow.

The coffee part was what we all looked forward to the most and often lasted longer than the meal itself because that was when we talked. Conversation was wide-ranging, starting with the day's happenings and branching off as things reminded us of other things. Sometimes it was serious, but most of it was hilarious (or so we thought). And the most hilarity happened at the wrong times.

It always started on Thursdays – choir night.

Most of our coffee chats were leisurely, but lively, with jovial gossip, jokes, puns, apt quotes, imitations, and all manner of good talk. On choir nights, however, they seemed to become uproarious and fast-paced. At least two, sometimes three of us had to leave shortly after eating, so we had to fit two hours into one, which made for a rather frenetic atmosphere. The jokes and puns had to happen as we ate, and all the news and talk had to fit into a condensed period while the singers gulped their coffee and ran.

This led to some rapid crosstalk, with the volume turned up, as everyone tried to get his points made or her quips heard. The singers then departed, reliving the previous half hour while enroute to church. Quite often we came up with better retorts or punch lines that we found hysterical. We re-argued the points, agreed and disagreed with opinions expressed, and generally kept the hectic mood flourishing.

When we arrived at choir practice, we were not in an appropriately earnest frame of mind. Almost anything would remind us of our table discussion and start us giggling, or worse, trying not to. The choir director was patient because she needed us, but we were disruptive, and we knew it. We would promise ourselves to do better each week, but we slipped up over and over. We simply could not keep Thursdays calm.

Much of our conversation was about books (big surprise, huh?). One memorable book we talked about was "*The Strange One*." It wasn't really memorable because of subject matter or theme or anything literary like that but because of the discourse it inspired. Mom was reading it in her snatched leisure time, and each night she reported the story "so far." Apparently, a migrating goose dropped to earth from his flock into a strange country and mated with a native goose. Paralleling the goose narration was the story of a wanderer and a local girl who fall in love. Come spring, when the geese flew back to their summer quarters and the weather improved so the man could wander on, the question was whether goose and guy had developed enough roots to stay put.

I am sure it was a good book. It sounded thoughtful and thematically interesting. Mom really enjoyed reading it and told us about it enthusiastically. But the discussion became a little irreverent for such a deep theme. Bobby came up with "Will the gander meander?" Dad asked if he would become a "loose goose." We tried to honk like geese. Bobby developed a mating call. Poor Mom, who was really wrapped up in the tale and really cared about the characters, couldn't help laughing, but I think we spoiled it for her. None of us recall how the book ended; we never knew the author's name; no one looked for it later, either on lists or library shelves. But we all remember the story and the fun it created.

I guess I should check it out some day.

The dictionary was always on the windowsill, ready for consultation because much of our conversation revolved around semantics – not that any of us knew what that meant. Mom probably did, but if we had asked, she would have told us to look it up.

Hence, the dictionary.

Many cups of coffee were spilled as it passed from hand to hand. Each of us tried to top the other with obscure words that had apt meanings, and words that could be both nouns and verbs. When I called some of the things we said "uncouth" Bobby and Dad promised (insincerely) to "couth it up." I objected, declaring it was not a verb, but the dictionary proved me wrong: it used to be, but was no longer used as such.

Bobby and Dad maintained they were being "classical."

When I was still a Girl Scout, I tried diligently to earn the badges the leaders were coaxing us to work on. Besides the usual Scout ones – camping, building a fire, cooking over it, swimming – I remember the "softer" skill badges, such as 'Housekeeping.' This involved planning nutritious meals, baking a cake, and setting a dinner table. For this last item, we all 'trooped' to Jane Bartley's beautiful Connecticut Avenue house where her mother taught us the proper way to set the table for a formal dinner: we learned that the knife blades were turned inward, the folded napkins went on the left, the salad fork was outside the dinner fork, the water glass was at the tip of the knife, and other esoterica.

We were to set our home dinner tables for a week using a check list she gave us, and which was to be turned in at the next meeting. I followed directions faithfully, even though we seldom used salad forks and drank coffee, not water, at meals. I used the good china and Mom's silver and cloth napkins. I placed the best glasses on the table along with the coffee mugs. Those spoiled the formality, but the family absolutely wouldn't give up coffee – even for a week.

It was certainly a positive reinforcement because I have never forgotten how to set a formal table and have used the knowledge often through the years. Back then, however, I found that it made the table more crowded and meant that we had more dishes to wash. The whole family was pleased when the week was over, the badge was earned, and things were back to normal.

FOR US, THAT IS.

FOOD

Mom didn't consider herself a cook. I honestly don't think she liked to cook! But many of her meals became classics and were demanded again and again.

A favorite cold-weather meal was a dish she called goulash. It consisted of ground beef, sliced potatoes, chopped onion and tomato soup – remarkably simple to make and heavenly to smell when coming in from a cold walk home. This was the casserole she served the first time my husband, Bob, came to dinner and officially entered the family. Bob's request for seconds and then thirds endeared him to her forever.

Another of our favorite foods was scalloped potatoes – not in general, but the way Mom made them. The key to the success of this dish was partly in the thickness of the potato slices and the amount of milk, but mostly in the secret ingredient – Velveeta cheese. That questionable dairy product was layered between the potatoes, and it melted into and flavored the milk which was absorbed into the slices. The dish came from the oven creamy and bubbly and browned on top. We most often had it with Canadian bacon, so it was a regular on our Easter dinner menu.

We were fortunate to have relatives who wintered in Florida. Each Christmas we received several huge boxes of fresh citrus fruit, and none of the contents went to waste. We had fruit and fresh orange juice for breakfast, of course, but Mom even created a dessert out of grapefruit halves. She loosened the sections, sprinkled the halves with brown sugar, topped them with a Maraschino cherry and placed them under the broiler until they bubbled. I don't know if Vitamin C really does keep colds away, but we had our daily doses and all of us stayed pretty healthy, winter after winter. Without a flu shot, too!

Spring and summer brought other Mom creations. Ambrosia, as we called it, introduced spring. When the strawberry man pushed his cart through the neighborhood, we got a concoction made of the berries, banana slices and sections of whatever citrus fruit was left in the Christmas boxes. Sometimes we had this with honey, and sometimes we had it plain. With honey, it was dessert; plain, it became a second 'vegetable.'

No one drank tea in our house, so during the humid summers we had iced coffee to cool off – with cream and sugar, which we didn't add when we drank it hot. We often drank this treat while we ate oat and chocolate bars that were just chocolate chip cookies without the fuss. Spread in a pan instead of dropped on a cookie sheet, they were quick and easy, and healthy, of course, because they had oatmeal in them.

Ice cream was a company dessert. Freezers were small in the '50s, so keeping ice cream on hand was not possible. When we wanted to serve it, we bought it, hand-packed, from the drug store just before dinner, or we sent someone down to Doc's to get it as we were clearing the table afterwards. Of the four flavor choices (vanilla, chocolate, strawberry, or Neapolitan), chocolate was our favorite, but if we got that, Mom wouldn't make Lumpy Chocolate Sauce, and that was the whole point of having ice cream!

I think the lumps were a mistake the first time. Maybe the chocolate didn't melt right, or she took the sauce off the burner too soon, or something. But when it was poured, hot, over the cold ice cream, the bitter lumps and the sweet ice cream tasted very intentional. After that first time, 'lumpy' became a positive adjective, and we requested that she leave some in each time she made the sauce.

Grandma Hattie often baked bread, filling the whole house with a wonderful warm, rich smell. The best part of a loaf, Dad always maintained, was the 'knust,' or the end slice, which had a crusty layer underneath, so the big gobs of butter didn't leak through. There were only two to each loaf, which resulted in arguments about who had got them last time. Dad usually commandeered at least one from each baking, while the other four of us competed for the rest of the end pieces that were left.

Mom never made bread. I don't think she was big on the fussiness of yeast baking, but she made an exception when Christmas came around. About two weeks before the holiday, she began to make, not cookies, but prune kuchen. This involved a jam of prunes and sugar spread between two thin layers of yeast dough. After baking, she drizzled white icing over the top, so it was sweet and tart and just the right taste for Christmas morning breakfast. We had it with our coffee as we opened our tree presents – a ritual that usually lasted until lunchtime.

Her other Christmas baking tradition was Cranberry Bread, a recipe that she got from the Ocean Spray fresh cranberry bag. This was a quick, not a yeast, bread that, again, had that sweet/tart flavor. The loaves were often given as Christmas presents or hostess gifts, but we always saved several for ourselves. After the midnight service on Christmas Eve, Mom topped slices with butter and toasted them under the broiler. We ate them as we filled each other's stockings with joke presents and candy.

Cranberry bread was truly seasonal, and still is, because fresh cranberries are only available in the late fall, in time for Thanksgiving. Each of us continues the cranberry bread custom. I still make multiple loaves and give them away to hard-to-shop-for friends and relatives, and we always keep a loaf or two for ourselves. Beth makes cranberry muffins which were a favorite of her father-in-law. Bob and Judy also make the loaves, but I think they are only for their own family breakfasts.

Mom's other creations also live on. Goulash (sometimes called Myra's Goop – another story) has been my dinner-in-a-hurry for years and was beloved by my teenage sons; we all make the scalloped potatoes whenever we have ham; we make grapefruit Mom's way, still – even for breakfast; and when I can't find chocolate chip ice cream, I attempt to make the lumpy sauce from her recipe.

THANKS MOM!

GROWING UP NIXON IN THE 1950'S

I never thought much about my name until 1952.

I was christened Suzanne, but everyone called me Susie, and that's how I thought of myself. SUSIE. S-U-S-I-E! Even though I had a legitimate right to put a Z in the middle of my nickname, it never occurred to me to deviate from the norm. Creative spelling didn't come along until fifty years later. The most creative I got with my name was to dot my I with a heart – in junior high, I think.

My mother wanted to name me after my grandmother, her mother. But Grandma Hattie put her foot down. She refused to "give a little baby the burdensome name 'Henrietta.'" My father preferred 'Marie,' my mother's name, or 'Irene' because he and Mom liked dancing to the current popular song "Goodnight, Irene." Mom vetoed both, 'Marie' because I "needed my own name" and 'Irene' because it would "date me" and "everyone would know how old" I was.

They compromised by giving me Marie as a middle name and coming up with another name, a 'French' one, as my first name. Had I been a boy, there would have been no discussion. I would have been Cleon Robert III after my father and grandfather. That honor went to my brother three years later.

The 1952 name awareness was concentrated on my last name – NIXON. In that year, Dwight David Eisenhower chose Richard M. Nixon to be his vice-presidential running mate, and overnight, my last name was in the news daily. No matter where I lived, I would have had questions about this, but we lived in a suburb of Washington DC!

The questions lasted for eight years: "Any relation?" "Are you related to____?" "Is it spelled the same as____?"

We all had a memorized reply involving brothers back in the 17th century and two branches of the family, which we recited mechanically. Even after the Eisenhower years, my parents and brother were answering questions about a name that had become notorious, but of which they were proud. My sister and I were able to avoid this by marrying and acknowledging our family pride with an N initial in our signatures. No one ever asked what the N stood for.

In the 1950's, however, my last name brought perks as well as questions. I was elected vice president of my sixth-grade class because of it. Jim O'Brien, politically and promotionally astute for his age, organized a campaign and "ran" me as VP, partly so that I wouldn't support his candidate's opposition— a boy I had a crush on—and partly because my name in the VP position was a natural publicity tool.

And, in 1957, a friend whose father was a journalist for the Evening Star newspaper, got two press passes for us, and we were able to get through the police lines and march alongside Eisenhower's second inaugural parade. I think Nancy was hoping I would say something to Dick and Pat as they drove by.

My mother enjoyed perks as well. Living in the choice suburb of Chevy Chase with the name of Nixon brought immediate service when she called for oil delivery or a question on a department store bill. One time she answered the phone to hear "Is this the Richards' residence?"

"No, I'm sorry," Mom replied. "This is the Nixon residence."

There was dead silence for a beat. Then a very apologetic and embarrassed voice said, "I am SO sorry Mrs. Nixon." There was a click before Mom could explain.

A dubious honor from this era was my listing in a school program as 'Pat Nixon' by an absent-minded high school music teacher. He produced "The Mikado" one year, and because of my time in Japan, he made me chairman of the costume committee. It was hard work to outfit ten leads and a fairly large chorus with Japanese-looking costumes, and I looked forward to acknowledgement of some kind. Alas, he always called me Miss Nixon in class and couldn't remember my first name. The only Nixon female he could think of was the vice president's wife. Even some of the cast came looking for 'Pat' when something was wrong or missing.

So -- if there are any Mrs. Richard Nixon biographers out there, I can point to a primary source that says Pat Nixon did costumes for the Bethesda-Chevy Chase High School production of "The Mikado" in 1958.

COUSINS

W e had eight cousins, the exact number as the title of one of my favorite books. Four of these were the daughters of Dad's brother, Uncle Bill Nixon, and his wife Aunt Polly, who lived on the "other side" of the Potomac River, in Vienna, Virginia – not too far for either family to come for a visit. Their names were Eloise, Nan, Pollyann, and Jane, and each of the older ones was just about a year younger than each of us, so we all had a special companion. Except Jane, who was younger than anyone by about six years.

We saw them regularly. Until Grandma Natalie died, we met for Thanksgivings and birthdays at the Peacock home in Washington DC, which was about halfway for each family. Thanksgivings were the traditional huge feasts with a children's table in an alcove and grownups in the dining room. After the pies were eaten, we kids would be sent upstairs to play in the spare room that had a trunk of old-fashioned clothing and lots of discarded knickknacks, while the adults had coffee and whatever. For us, that was the best part – after pumpkin pie, of course.

Birthdays were always double celebrations. Grandma N baked two cakes, one chocolate and one white, and we celebrated my birthday and Eloise's together in the winter (both Pisces) and Bobby's and Nan's in the fall (both Libra). There was the usual argument about whose cake was chocolate and whose 'plain,' and it most often ended up not mattering because nothing was left of them after the parties.

It was just at candle-blowing time that it made any difference.

Christmas was another get-together time. Sometimes we went south, and sometimes they all came to us. If they came north, Eloise and/or Nan usually stayed over; when they did, our favorite game was 'beauty shop.' We would wash our hair and Mom would set it. We would paint each other's nails and practice putting on lipstick. We even let Beth join in the fun although she was much younger. Bobby held himself aloof from this, but everyone joined in the games and the reading aloud and the playing school that went on throughout the visit.

When we went down to their house, the visits were full of riotous noise and messy wrappings and very late dinners because Aunt Polly usually forgot to put the ham in the oven until late afternoon. We learned to eat before we left so that we could join in all the fun without hunger pangs.

It was here that we saw the rest of our eight cousins – four boys who were the children of Aunt Polly's sister, Jane Harding. Their names were Ken, Rick, Bruce, and Vic. The oldest three were close in age to Eloise, Nan, Bobby, and me, so there were a lot of friendly arguments, playful fights, and good-natured teasing. The Harding boys made the long waits for dinner pass quickly.

Both the Hardings and the Bill Nixons had summer houses at Herald Harbor MD on the shore of the Severn River, so on summer weekends we pleaded with Mom and Dad to "take us to the beach, puh-leeze." We knew that when we got there, we would be invited to stay, and, generally, at least one of us did. These visits lasted longer than a few days – usually until Mom and Dad drove over again the following Sunday.

During the week, no one dared get in our way: we were "family-strong!" Seven or eight of us used to go to the village en masse and overwhelm the ice cream shop or the soda fountain with orders. We would then walk shoulder to shoulder down the sidewalk, enjoying the fact that people stepped aside when they saw us coming.

It helped that Kenny, Aunt Jane's eldest, went with us. He was tall and handsome and served as a page in the US Senate. Eloise and I were delighted to have him as our protector. Once we were even able to 'gamble' at the slot machines. It was illegal for us, but Kenny was old enough according to Eastern Shore laws at that time (or so he maintained), so he stood behind us while we pulled the handles of the one-armed-bandits. Only once! We won some money and had a thrill. That was enough. I don't believe I ever told Mom and Dad.

I think the Severn River was our first swimming pool. Because there was a polio epidemic, and, probably more important, because Mom didn't really like to swim, I don't remember seeing a pool or even knowing that public pools existed. So, the river was our first introduction to big water (that is, deeper than a bathtub) and the need to float in it. It was also our first encounter with tides.

A large rock sitting in the water not far from Aunt Polly's beach was our paddling goal when we first learned to swim. It was just distant enough to be good practice, with shallow spots on the way to put our feet down when our arms got tired. The sun warmed the rock so that we could rest on it soaking wet and not be cold.

Once, when Bobby and I reached it, we felt safe and happy – until the tide came in! Suddenly, the beach was much further away, we couldn't see the bottom anymore, and when I slid off to swim back, I got water up my nose and panicked. I struggled back up to Bobby, and we both called for help.

It seemed an eternity before a grown-up came to our rescue. I don't remember who it was. He escorted us back one at a time, making us swim all the way – to help us overcome our fear, I suppose. That evening we got a lesson in tidal cycles and 'safety in the water' rules that we never forgot. The rock remained our favorite spot for a long time, but as we grew, it seemed to get smaller and smaller, and the distance to it became shorter and shorter.

We spent many summers there with our eight cousins. We all took the Red Cross lifesaving lessons when we were fourteen. We went sailing, tacking close to the course used by the Naval Academy midshipmen in order to wave at those handsome guys. We dug our heels in sand looking for clams and hung bait off the end of the pier to catch crabs. At night, newspapers were spread on the picnic table, the seafood was boiled in a big pot, and we sat and ate until it was gone. There was no table to clear or dishwashing afterward. We just rolled up the mess and threw it away. I was all for that kind of housekeeping.

There was a summer when we talked Mom and Dad into renting a house at Herald Harbor for a week, or maybe two. It had no beach, but it was up the road from Aunt Polly's, so we could walk down there and swim. Aunt Polly had rented half of her house to a family whose father was doing his two-week military reserve service at Ft. Meade. This family, from Altoona PA had two teenage girls and one rather sickly little boy. Debbie and Juanita fit right into our age group and that made our gang even more formidable when we went to the village. We became almost a secret society with hand signs that sent messages no one else could decipher and a kind of speech code that we used in front of the grown-ups.

One night, we planned to have a slumber party, which our respective parents had refused to allow. Debbie and Juanny were going to sneak into Eloise and Nan's room, and I was to wait until Mom and Dad were asleep and come down the road. But Mom was reading a good book and wouldn't turn out her light. I kept reading my own book until I couldn't keep my eyes open any more.

I fell asleep for I don't know how long and woke up in the dark of early morning. Since I had slept in my clothes, I was able to slip out and run down to Aunt Polly's. All was dark. I'd missed it!

I went back home and finished my night's sleep. Mom was surprised that I was already dressed when she got up.

"I thought you'd be tired this morning," she said. "You read for so <u>long</u> last night! It must have been a good book."

Debbie and Juanny also commented.

"Where were you? We waited until two, but you never came."

My guess is that Mom knew something was up and stayed awake deliberately. We never discussed it, but I can be suspicious too!

Our cousins remain on our Christmas card lists, but we have drifted apart and hardly ever get together all at once. We live in different states, and some of us have lived in foreign countries, so reuniting has been difficult. Several of us were at Nan's wedding to Hans Flinch in Copenhagen where I saw Pollyann and Kenny and got to room with Aunt Polly. That was forty years ago!

More recently, I met with Jane and Nan in Washington DC while I was attending my 50th high school reunion. And once we stopped in San Antonio to see Pollyann who had retired from her army career there. But we haven't been together as a gang since, probably, 1963.

Family feeling never goes away, however. I'm sure that we'd pick up where we left off if we were able to be all together again.

WE MIGHT EVEN PLAY BEAUTY SHOP!

THE THEATER GENE

M y sons once asked me if my sister was an angel.
"Umm - sometimes," I answered cautiously. "Why?"

"Because she is on our Christmas card," they said.

My sister Beth had appeared in the Omaha Playhouse production of *A Christmas Carol* for several years and was a prominent figure on one of the Christmas cards the Playhouse sold as a fundraiser. Our Christmas cards usually had religious figures on them, and knowing that my sister was not named Mary, they figured she had to be one of the Heavenly Host.

Their question started me thinking about the Nixon theater genes. I don't know where these genes come from, but they must be from somewhere because we all have them - in such abundance, in fact, that they have been handed down to the next two generations.

Mom sang and played piano but had no real urge to perform. Instead, she anchored the alto section of the church choir and played for us when we sang at home. Dad sang enthusiastically and off-key during church services, and there were rumors that he was part of a jazz group in his wild younger years – a sort of Rat Pack ensemble, I think. But neither seemed to have had any inclination, and perhaps no time, to follow up on these beginnings.

I don't remember their going to many plays or even movies, and music concerts were pretty much limited to church events. Any exposure we children had to live performance was confined to school productions or occasional times when Aunt Ruth insisted that we see a certain cultural icon like The Nutcracker ballet. So how we all got involved in the world of theater I have no idea.

Beth became the most professional of us three. She persisted with piano study – something I gave up in junior high. She also took voice lessons and sang in several choral groups during high school. After majoring in music education and discovering that her students mostly took her courses for an easy A, she switched to managing offices for regional theaters and fund drives for local performing arts organizations. Along the way she sang in choruses for musicals and took hard-to-fill roles in plays.

Brother Bob went a different route, writing plays for Renaissance Fairs and other events, skits for church functions, and, once, a TV script covering the history of the Bible in one hour. He liked dressing up and playing roles like the Cowardly Lion at parties, remaining in character much as Civil War reenactors do when they maintain they don't know about 9/11. However, his strength was directing, and for years he guided middle schoolers through some very ambitious shows.

As the least talented in all ways, I mostly worked backstage – scenery, props, costumes, and anything else that would let me be involved in the theater world. I read plays for fun, and my favorite teaching units were the drama ones; I used plays in my overseas' English classes to help students pronounce our language with less inhibition. AND – I passed the gene to my son Bryan who studied musical theater performance in college. He spent the first ten years of his working life appearing on professional stages and entertaining on a cruise ship before switching to a more secure career as a postal worker.

Our son Bob went the scientific route, but his wife and children were involved in music and theater performance, roping him in as well. Once they all appeared in *A Christmas Story* as a family activity. His children continued their musical pursuits through their college years and now, as they settle in different places, look for opportunities to involve themselves in various performing activities.

Where this desire for exhibition originated still remains a mystery. It might be a coincidence, but no matter what the answer is, the trend will continue. Brother Bob's three grandchildren, ranging in age from 16 to 11, annually dance in *The Nutcracker*, along with their mother (my niece), the older boy's hobby is creating plays and corralling friends and family into acting them out while he films them, and the youngest, Evelyn, has begun to write books and movie scripts.

THE BEAT GOES ON.

IF THE PEW SHAKES

R ichard Sage didn't get up! He was <u>supposed</u> to. The bulletin clearly stated that a candle would be lighted when we sang *Angels from the Realms of Glory.*

Let me explain.

Our pastor liked non-traditional worship services and was especially creative during the holidays. On this particular Christmas Eve, the beloved story of Christ's birth was to be told using carols along with Bible verses. Each carol would be accompanied by the lighting of a candle. Two acolytes were recruited to do this on cue. One was Richard Sage.

We had already sung *O Come, O Come Emmanuel* (Candle #1), *O Little Town of Bethlehem* (Candle #2), and *Away in a Manger* (Candle #3). Now we had reached the shepherd part and were halfway through the first verse of *Angels.*

Nothing happened. There was an uncomfortable stir in the choir – not too much – just a flutter. They knew the script, and someone (Richard Sage? The Other One?) wasn't following it. As the second verse progressed, some in the congregation began to notice lack of activity. Paper rustled as people checked their bulletins. Yes, something should be happening. Was Richard asleep? – it **was** late. There were two acolytes: did he not know it was his turn?

As the second chorus of "Come and worship" arrived, even the minister looked uncomfortable. Was there something wrong with the candle-lighting tool? Had he not explained the procedure well enough?

The congregation started to sing the third verse, and all of a sudden, Richard Sage bounded up. In two strides he reached the altar and lit his candle. As he returned to his seat, the congregation released its collective breath and relaxed in relief – except in the Nixon pew. We were trying, without much success, to suppress laughter without snorting.

Even now, none of us can sing this hymn without a smile. If we are together the pew trembles with muffled giggles. Why?

Richard was right on cue – planned or unplanned. The beginning line of the third verse of *Angels from the Realms of Glory* is—

SAGES LEAVE YOUR CONTEMPLATIONS

He did!

CALVARY LUTHERAN CHURCH

?? ---------- DO YOU REMEMBER ---------- ??

1. DIAL PHONES

The telephone stood in the living room, at the foot of the stairs and below the doorbell chimes. When you answered, you were tethered to it by a cord that wasn't very long. But the good location meant that if the call were lengthy, you could at least sit down and talk. Also, two shallow steps up from the living room was a landing with a coat closet – handy to crawl into in case the conversation was "private."

Nearness to the chimes was handy too, especially for Mom. A talkative friend used to keep her on the line for an hour or more, so when we got home from school, Mom would often motion to us to ring the doorbell. When we did, she would leap up and say, "Someone's at the door. I need to go." This worked for a while, but Tobey (the friend) soon got wise and said, "Go ahead, I can hang on." Cordless phones, or better still, caller ID, sure would have helped.

2. NAMING THE BABY

Beth was born a week before Christmas, so Bobby and I were eager to name her something seasonal. We put our heads together and came up with several Christmas-y name suggestions.

"Let's call her 'Holly'," I said.

"I think it should be 'Carol'," said Bobby, "like a Christmas carol."

I concurred because I had been reading a sentimental story called "*The Bird's' Christmas Carol*" about a child named Carol who died on Christmas Eve listening to her namesakes sung by a church choir.

We also thought of 'Mary" for obvious reasons, and 'Noelle' because of "born is the King..."

Mom and Dad had already decided on Elizabeth (Mom's middle name) and Ruth (for Aunt Ruth from Dad's side of the family), so when we rushed up to the bedroom with our list, Mom explained that the name had already been chosen.

"But she is a Christmas baby," we begged. "She needs a Christmas name."

"Well, we don't have to call her Liz or Betty," Mom said. "We can call her Beth. That is like Bethlehem where Jesus was born."

Bobby and I talked it over and finally agreed that that name would be fine, so she became and remained Beth. I can't imagine her as anything else.

3. JOSEPHINE LOWMAN'S 9-DAY DIET

It was a spring ritual. As soon as the final stale jellybean disappeared from the last Easter basket, we all — well, Mom — decided we had to "get back in shape." Most of the time this meant losing weight although Bobby and I sometimes did half-hearted calisthenics on weekends.

J-Lo's diet promised a five-to-ten-pound loss in nine days IF you followed her regimen EXACTLY. We always started on a Monday with good intentions to "stick with it" as Jo exhorted on page 2 of her little pink booklet. I usually began by imagining myself in a Sandra Dee or Annette Funicello dress and promising myself a shopping trip on Day 10.

The diet depended a lot on skim milk, half-cup portions of vegetables (do you **know** how many peas are in a ½ cup?!) and thin, dry — meaning no butter or jelly — slices of toast. No salt, no sugar, no gravy, and no dessert. For nine days! Treats came every couple days. Treats — HAH: tomato juice (?), two or three olives (??), ½ cup of fresh fruit (a little better). Otherwise, the week and a half were pretty stark.

Did it work? I maybe lost three or four pounds, but I might have cheated just a <u>little.</u> It's hard to watch your friends eat ice cream and not even have a taste! And Josephine said not to add <u>anything</u>.

As far as I know none of us except Mom had much success, and after nine days, with a deep sigh of relief, we returned without guilt to buttered toast, mashed potatoes, and coca cola after school.

Until next spring.

    4. MEMORIZATION

We all did it. It even <u>used</u> to be a learning strategy! Think:

> The Alphabet Song
>
> The Times Tables
>
> The Periodic Table
>
> Shakespeare Sonnets (or parts of them)
>
> Lines from class plays

Aside from academics, though, I think our generation memorized a lot just for fun. My childhood recollections are sometimes fuzzy and incomplete, and they come sporadically.

But give me one line of verse or music from the '40's or early '50's, and I could probably recite the entire piece. Here are some beginnings that came to mind as I was typing this introduction:

    A. How do you like to go up in a swing

        Up in the air so blue?

B. When I looked out the window

    Of the house beside the mill

C. Goodbye dear Little Old Lady

    So good, so sweet, so true.

D. Jesus loves me, this I know

E. Now I lay me down to sleep

    I pray the Lord my soul to keep

F. Hurray, Horree, Harrah, Harrum

    It's Arthur and Celeste

G. When I was sick and lay abed,

    I had two pillows at my head

H. They're changing guard at Buckingham Palace.

    Christopher Robin went down with Alice.

Just in case you think I don't remember the rest, here are the endings of the verses (but not the complete poems or songs— not enough room). I didn't look them up either! Who needs Google?

a. Oh, I do think it's the pleasantest thing

Ever a child can do.

(The Swing by Robert Louis Stevenson)

b. I saw a scarlett alligator

Sitting on a hill.

c. You know an elephant never forgets,

And I'll come back to you.

(Babar, the Little Elephant record by Paul Wing)

d. For the Bible tells me so.

Little ones to Him belong.

They are weak, but He is strong.

(Anna B. Warner)

e. I pray the Lord my soul to keep.

If I should die before I wake,

I pray the Lord my soul to take.

(The New England Primer)

f. Of all the little elephants,

I like my cousins best.

(see c)

g. And all my toys around me lay

To keep me happy all the day.

(The Land of Counterpane by RLS)

h. That's all I know. It probably came from one of the British children's books I was always reading.

++

Nothing I learned later (except maybe excerpts from *Luther's Small Catechism* and some Robert Frost poems) has stuck with me the way these pieces have. Should we encourage "learning by heart" once more?

5. DRIVING ARM SIGNALS

We were encouraged ('allowed' might be a better word) to stick our arms out of the windows! It was part of learning to drive. Even as children we "helped" Dad by signaling from the back seat: arm straight out for a left turn; arm bent toward the roof for a right one; a dangling arm for slowing or stopping. Whoever sat on the right side of the car did the same things except the opposite way—arm straight out was a right turn; arm bent up at the elbow, a left one. We used these on our bicycles too, even if there were no riders behind us. We felt so important and responsible doing it. We were keeping others safe!

Blinking light turn signals weren't standard on cars until the mid-1950's, and they certainly weren't on the cars we drove because our first few were used cars; thus, we still made use of our arms during our high school years. We weren't the only ones who kept using the arm gestures either. It took a while for drivers to look at the rear bumpers of cars for other motorists' intentions, so arm signals continued until well into the 1960's.

Modern drivers can still catch glimpses of their usefulness. Motorcyclists, and sometimes even truck drivers, signal with their arms on streets and interstates if roads are particularly crowded. BE ALERT!

6. *CHILDREN'S ACTIVITIES* AS *HIGLIGHTS* USED TO BE CALLED

This magazine was our Sesame Street.

Like today's magazine, it had stories and photos of children from other countries, articles on school and health from a child point of view, and regular pages of crafts and activities – all geared to the 5-9-year age range. A relative gave us a subscription for several years, and we eagerly awaited its arrival each month. In the first place, it was exciting to have the mailman bring something just for us. But mostly, we looked forward to the fun it contained.

Not all of it required reading. A favorite each month was the "Hidden Pictures" page. A beautiful and busy black-and-white drawing contained hidden images of a list of things at the bottom of the page. Accompanying the word of each hidden object was a picture of it, but not necessarily identical to what was hidden. So, a rabbit might be curled up next to the word but hopping in the hidden picture. This absorbed us for hours, and it still challenged us even after we had found everything because the overall picture was so interesting and distracting that we forgot where the hidden items were.

Another page offered advice on manners via two characters named Goofus and Gallant. At first, they were stick figures, then cartoons, and finally real-looking drawings of two boys. I remember Gallant looking blond, neatly dressed, and smiling. Goofus, however, was always angry and ill-kempt, and had dark hair.

Covered were such occasions as 'helping mother,' 'holding doors for people,' 'assisting the elderly across a street,' and 'being cheerful when disappointed.' Side-by-side pictures showed Gallant doing things properly and Goofus rebelling. We both wanted to behave like Gallant, but I don't think we liked him much. We thought Goofus looked like he was more fun, and besides, we often <u>felt</u> more like him than Gallant.

There were many other features that were fun and informative. Like the Sesame Street program on TV in the '60's, this magazine taught us without our knowing it. It is heartening to see the magazine still in print – and in color. (Ours was in black and white throughout because color printing was expensive and difficult to produce.) Childhood literacy needs all the help it can get – in print, not on screen!

7. DRINKING FROM THE HOSE

It was <u>hot</u> in Chevy Chase during the summer! Hot inside; hot outside; especially hot in our bedrooms; even hot under the trees, though, at least, we were in the shade. With no air-conditioning in houses, we played outside on most days – even in August when the wimpy Congress took a vacation to escape the heat. After all, it wasn't <u>much</u> hotter than inside.

Such intense and enduring heat parched lawns and gardens, so most houses had hoses handily coiled in flower beds or behind bushes to sprinkle plants and grass during the relative cool of the evening. After dinner, fathers or older children would be seen wandering around their properties watering greenery.

The hoses were used in the daytime too, but not on plants. If your mom said, "Go and get some fresh air," you knew you should probably get out of the house. So, we played outside. In the heat. Even when we played quiet games in the shade, we got sweaty and thirsty. Without the convenience of paper or plastic cups, and without the ubiquitous water bottles of today, we had two options. We could go to the back door and ask for a drink of water; we had to stand there and drink it, though. It was too dangerous to carry a glass around, and messy too, sometimes.

Or - we could quench our thirst with the hose. An intrepid playmate would wade gingerly into the garden area, uncoil part of the hose, and turn on the water. All of us would then take turns drinking from the nozzle and squirting each other. No one was concerned about sanitation then, and I never heard of anyone getting sick from drinking hose water.

Mom usually allowed this for a while, and we usually returned the hose to the garden and turned the water off. But at least one time during each summer, we forgot. Unless Mom took care of it, Dad would come home from work to find a flooded garden and mud puddles by the azaleas. We were lectured about waste, and the scolding didn't end that day, either. We got more when the water bill came.

In our defense, though, we DID save him some work. He didn't have to water the garden for several evenings.

8. SUNDAY CLOTHES

We never wore sneakers to church or jeans to school! Our clothes had specific purposes – play, school, church, party, cleaning the garage.... So did our shoes although there was some overlap there. You could wear church shoes to parties and sometimes school shoes to church (if you weren't acolyting or wearing a choir robe). But mostly, we had separate apparel for different activities.

Play clothes were usually discarded school clothes such as slightly stained jerseys (as we called T-shirts) or faded skirts and mended dresses that still "had some life left" in them.

School clothes were purchased in September – a basic wardrobe of neutral skirts/trousers and several tops that coordinated with the bottoms. I remember wearing a lot of plaid and was especially fond of a Black Watch plaid, accordion-pleated skirt with which I could wear navy, green, and yellow tops. I hated outgrowing that one because it made me look slim and grown up.

Our best clothes were an investment, bought to last - hopefully for a number of seasons - by changing accessories like hats, gloves, and shoes. A dress with a jacket would do for church in the winter with a felt hat and dark shoes and become an Easter outfit by changing the hat to a straw one and wearing patent leather heels. These were the clothes we were supposed to change as soon as we got home. Not so much the school clothes: we could go outside in them as long as we changed our shoes.

Party clothes were different from church clothes – perhaps frillier, more colorful, slightly more frivolous. You could overlap church clothes with party clothes, but not vice versa. Party clothes were inappropriate for worship!

Dress codes were both stated and unstated. Schools had dress codes written into their handbooks – closed-toed shoes, appropriately modest apparel, no jeans, no slacks for girls. Church attire depended on parents and your age. Boys usually started wearing ties at age 7 or 8 and jackets when they began junior high (middle school to you). Girls wore hats from age 7 on.

Party clothes were chosen by subtle peer pressure. If everyone had a circular skirt and six crinolines, that was what you wanted too. In eighth grade, the day of our fall dance, a girl in my class (named Beverly – I will never forget her) wore the exact same skirt that I had for the dance. To school!! My new party outfit!! She was taller and slimmer than I was, too, so she looked better in it. I was so disappointed.

There seem to be no rules about proper apparel anymore, and it is hard to decide what to wear on any occasion. I often find myself overdressed at church and too informal for lunches with the girls. I simply can't bring myself to pair denim and gold jewelry, or lace and shorts. While it is easier to get dressed in a hurry, it is harder to know what to choose.

9. HURRICANES WERE ONLY GIRLS

Boys didn't get to be storms until 1979. Up to then hurricanes were named after girls in alphabetical order. Only hurricanes! Snowstorms and tornadoes didn't have names.

Living inland, in the mid-Atlantic area, meant that our storms were usually in the Connie to Janet name range because our storm season was generally August and September. No matter how they affected our coastal towns, they were an exciting break in our inland routine.

Hurricane Hazel, in 1954, was the most memorable and established our personal hurricane experience and regimen. The school year had started when Hazel developed, and we were dismissed before lunch. Our school district had no school buses (hardly any did, actually), so we were all on our own to get home before she hit. I remember navigating Connecticut Avenue without crossing guards and being stranded on the grassy boulevard in the middle while the wind blew in circles and cars whizzed by. Obviously, workplaces had been dismissed early, too.

Finally home, I scurried to help bring in trash cans, secure the swings in the back yard and fasten the garage doors tightly. Mom always made a pot of coffee and cooked something that could be eaten cold in case the electricity went out. And we brought in kindling and a couple of logs so we could build a fire if it got chilly. (And even if it didn't!)

We then hunkered down with books and schoolwork and slippers and sewing (for Mom) and waited for Hazel to strike. When she came, it got dark outside, and the wind seemed to attack the house. The rain on the windows was so loud and constant that we kept checking to see if any panes were cracked. When we looked out, we saw trees bending, even our oak tree in the front, and leaves flew around in a circles like small bats. It was frightening, but fascinating, and we had to be reminded constantly to stay away from the windows.

Electricity did go out, so we ate our meals in the living room and popped corn over the fire and read by sitting in its shafts of light. We played word games and talked and took naps and felt snug and warm and safe despite the angry weather outdoors. We were actually disappointed when the storm moved on and the electricity was restored. Going upstairs to bed seemed like an excursion to an unknown country after our cozy time before the fire.

I don't remember another storm as bad as Hazel even though we had a Connie and a Diane and a Janet during my school days. We also had some false alarms where we prepared for the worst and only got a half hour downpour. Even though we built a fire and ate in the living room those times, there wasn't the same secure and comforting feeling without the outside threat.

I ACTUALLY REMEMBER HURRICANES FONDLY.

10. PIG LATIN

We used to enjoy speaking this 'foreign' language, and I often wished that the real Latin had such few rules! The basic idea was to take the consonant sound from the beginning of the word and put it at the end with an 'ay' sound attached. (EX: "Ere-hay omes-cay uh-thay us-bay" = "Here comes the bus.") At first it was difficult to do this quickly, but we all got pretty fluent after a while. We used to work on the skill and use it whenever it was appropriate – and sometimes when it wasn't.

A genre of this vernacular was the swapping of consonant sounds from word to word, sort of the academic Pig Latin version because it took more thought and practice. We got quite good at this also. Bobby liked to recite *The Midnight*

Ride of Paul Revere this way – with emphasis and gestures. It was always a hit:

> "Chisten my *lildren and who shall year, of the ridnight mide of Vaul Repere.*
>
> *On the Apteenth of Atril in Feventy Sive, Mardly a han is now alive*
>
> *To remember that yaymous fay and dear*
>
> *Of the ridnig*ht mide of Vaul Repere."

Well, you get the idea. He could recite the whole poem that way. Except the "house to house part.

YOU CAN'T TURN THAT AROUND!

Questions From Evelyn

What?

    Who?

        When?

            Why?

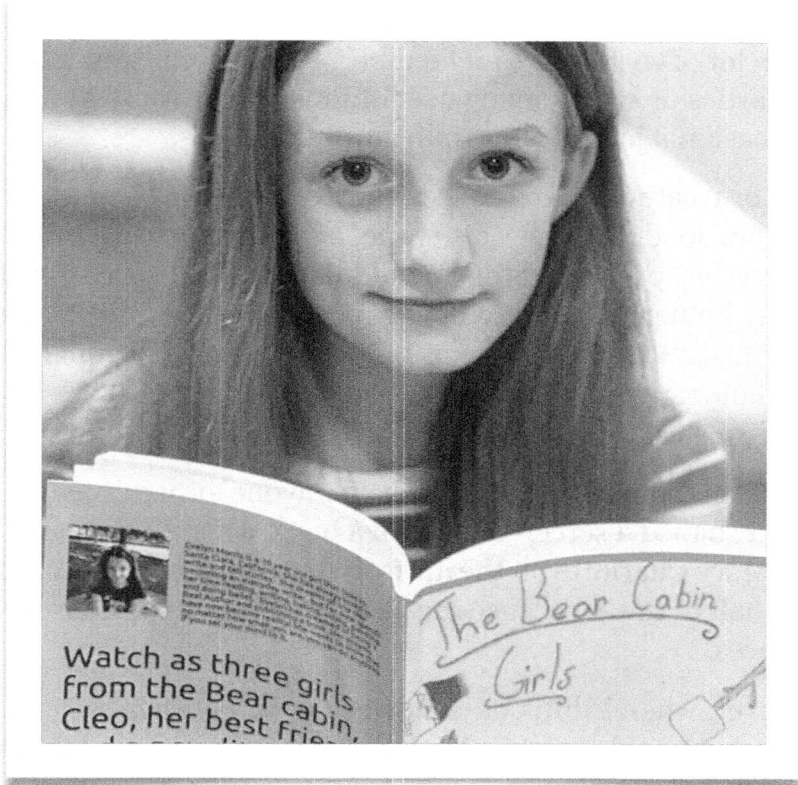

EVELYN, 2021

My 2020 Christmas present to my family members was a manuscript of this book, and my niece and her family read it aloud during their usual before-bed story hour. Her youngest child, Evelyn, began writing me letters asking for more information on certain incidents that intrigued her; we thus began a correspondence that has lasted to this day. I promised her that I would make a special section in the book for her questions and my replies.

Evelyn has begun writing herself, and she already has published two books. She was 11 years old in 2021!

What Halloween costumes did you have as a kid?

Halloween wasn't a big deal when I was a child, so I don't have a lot of costumes to remember. I don't recall going to any parties or seeing many decorations either; well - maybe an occasional jack-o-lantern in a window.

Trick or treating was a low-key activity and limited to the neighborhood. We knew everyone, and they knew us, even though they pretended they "couldn't guess!" The treats were usually homemade and seldom candy: chocolate chip cookies at Millards; Rice Krispy treats at Martins; chewing gum at Clevelands; there was even a dentist who gave out toothbrushes!

I don't remember playing a trick on anyone either except once. I soaped a screen door with a big X when I went out with Mary Charlotte on the air force base in Japan. We each did a half of the X because the people slammed the door in our faces.

However, when I think of Halloween now, I always remember the clown suit. Mom made it for me when I was about 5. It was bright red with sprinkles of flowers and triangles in yellow and blue and orange, and it had a white pleated collar like a ruff. Mom stiffened some of the red material and created a cone-shaped hat that was edged with yellow felt and tied under my chin.

I wore this costume for years because Mom's depression-era thrift "allowed for growth." So, I never actually outgrew the costume, but I did outgrow the desire to be a clown – in 5th grade, I think. It was passed on to Bobby, and he wore it several more years. It lasted well into the '70's when my own boys each wore it at least once.

In 5th grade I wore one of our kimonos, I believe, and in 6th grade I was a cowgirl! By that time, I was babysitting for 25 cents an hour, and I saved up to buy a costume kit with a 'leather' skirt and vest with fringe and a cowboy hat. Bobby lent me his cap guns and the holster, so I was very authentic! I remember the Halloween parade at school that year. I was really proud of my costume because it was "bought" and not homemade.

After grade school, when most of my friends were twelve, we didn't go trick or treating unless it was for a good cause. In 1950 the United Nations started a fund drive called "Trick or Treat for UNICEF," and a club I belonged to in junior high as well as the Girl Scout troop I was a member of were both supporting the effort. My friends and I went out together to various houses with the boxes that the UN supplied and asked people to put money in the box instead of giving us treats. Lots of them gave us both, so it was still a good night for us personally, but supporting this cause made us feel very grown up.

By ninth grade, it was understood that you were too old to go from house to house on October 31st. It was not cool! (Not that we had that expression then). However, it was okay to go with a younger sibling – just in case, you know! So, I sometimes tagged along with Bobby to 'protect' him. He didn't need it or want me to go, so I didn't do it very often.

Later, in a somewhat motherly way, I made the rounds with Beth.

Like I said at the beginning, Halloween wasn't the holiday it is now.

DO YOU THINK I MISSED SOMETHING?

Summer 1948

PLAYING ON SWING SET IN THE BACK YARD OF 6505 FULTON STREET IN CHEVY CHASE MD IN THE CLOWN SUIT

1948

What was your favorite birthday that you had?

Bobby always had the best birthdays. Beth and I had winter birthdays – hers a week before Christmas, mine usually during Lent. Neither date lent itself to elaborate personal festivities. But Bobby's was near the end of September, usually with good weather and not so far into the school year that we were swamped with homework. It was a perfect time to celebrate big time!

We usually took a family excursion to a place of Bobby's choice, often with several friends of his in tow. We either took a picnic or ate in a restaurant enroute, and, naturally, we visited an ice cream stand for double-decker cones on the way home.

Most often, Bobby chose to go to Ft. McHenry outside Baltimore MD or to the battlefield in Gettysburg PA because of his fascination with historical warfare, especially the Civil War.

The now-peaceful green battlefield of Gettysburg didn't mean much to me. I would look out from the top of the hill and try to visualize the fighting as Bobby described the lines of gray and blue-clad soldiers and explained the strategy. Sometimes he and his friends even reenacted parts of the battles. But I still didn't get it.

The war maps in the museum didn't help much either. They were full of X's and triangles and curved lines supposedly showing the advances and retreats, but I simply couldn't picture it. The rest of the museum was interesting, though. There were cases of uniforms and guns and black and white photos of men standing outside tents, and there were plaques with battle timelines, diary entries, and a whole section on the Gettysburg Address – which we memorized and practiced on the way home.

My own birthdays were mostly family affairs. For the early ones, we used to gather at Grandma Natalie's on Harrison Street in Washington DC. My cousin Eloise and I usually celebrated together, and she always seemed to get the chocolate birthday cake. Even though I was given a piece to eat, I still felt it was unfair. Presents were kind of disappointing too. Family members always gave me clothes, most of which didn't fit, or that I didn't like but had to wear the next time we got together.

Mom also invited the neighborhood kids in for cake and ice cream during the afternoon. Unlike at Grandma Natalie's, the cake was always chocolate and had lots of frosting because I liked the frosting better than the cake. We had vanilla ice cream, and each child took home a small crepe paper basket filled with candy. I don't remember any presents from these parties, but there must have been some. I do remember playing 'Pin the tail on the donkey' once. I think I pinned his tail on his ear!

As I grew older, the afternoon celebrations became more important to me than the family dinners. Guests included my schoolmates, and the presents were exciting – Nancy Drew books, 45rpm records, trading cards[2], and autograph albums were standard and much appreciated. These parties ended with talk and music and sometimes dancing, and I started reading one of the gift books as soon as the last guest closed the front door.

Once I invited three friends to my birthday dinner with the family in our house. One was a schoolmate, and the other two were neighborhood girls. On the evening before my birthday, just as we were bringing in the food for a "leftover" supper, the doorbell rang. When I opened the door, there stood Carol Carpenter – one of the neighborhood friends. She was all dressed up and carried a wrapped package. I just stood there, dumbfounded.

"Good evening," she said formally, breaking the silence.

---

[2] Trading cards were single picture cards from a regular deck. Sometimes these were jokers from our parents' bridge decks, but often they were from packs of assorted cards sold in dime stores. We girls would carry our collections to school and trade at recess. Most of us had shoe boxes with the cards sorted by category – flowers, people, famous paintings, etc. – and we would show off our newest acquisitions and then say, "Want to trade?" Cutthroat bargaining then took place, and sometimes friendships were spoiled (for a while) over a ruthless swap.

I looked frantically at Mom. Carol was obviously here for the dinner party a day early. "What should I do now?" I silently screamed.

Mom bustled up and ushered her in. Carol saw that she had come on the wrong night and was sheepishly crestfallen, but Mom wouldn't let her be ashamed for long.

"Come in and take off your coat," she said. "We are having leftovers tonight so that the refrigerator has room for the goodies tomorrow. You can help us clear it out."

We set another place at the table, and Carol joined in our usual dinnertime hilarity, shedding her self-conscious feelings as we ate our way through the bits and bobs of food. She gave me a 45rpm record of "The Ballad of Davy Crockett" that introduced the TV show, which was a favorite of mine at the time. And she came back the next day for the real celebration, so I had two parties that year.

By the time I was in junior high school, Beth was old enough to sit still during dinner, so the yearly milestones were often honored at a restaurant. We had two special places we liked to go. One was Brook Farm, and one was Normandie Farms. Despite the similarity of their names, they were quite different in atmosphere and menu, so it was up to the birthday child to choose the venue.

Brook Farm was the choice most often because it was only three blocks away and we could walk there. It wasn't too dressy either, so we could make a last-minute decision and still have time for homework on a school night. Besides, it was near Doc's Drugstore where we could pick up a quart of ice cream to eat later (after Mom made lumpy chocolate sauce, of course).

We ate other big-event dinners there also – graduations, confirmations, anniversaries -- and it served typical

American food, so we took our frequent foreign guests there to introduce them to fried chicken and French fries. The owner got to know us and seldom refused us a reservation, even if we called at the last minute (or just showed up).

Normandie Farms was about a half-hour drive away, so a dinner there was always planned ahead of time. We had to dress in our best and reserve a table and make sure we had an entire evening free because a meal there was an EVENT!

The waitresses dressed in the folk costumes of Normandy in France - full skirts with aprons and high headdresses that we couldn't figure out how they kept on their heads. The menu was full of French dishes that we couldn't pronounce, but they looked so pretty and tasted so good that we didn't mind. We reserved these dinners for reunions with people we hadn't seen for a long time, milestone birthdays, and college graduations – really special occasions.

Both restaurants, although changed in appearance, still exist, and I have been to each of them fairly recently. One has changed its name; both have changed in appearance; menus have been updated; but the food is still excellent and the nostalgia I feel when I go is very real.

COSTUMES FROM NORMANDY, FRANCE

Did you ever take part in plays or ballet performances? Were you ever a part of a Girl Scout troop or did you ever do any big projects for the community with your friends?

The short answer to both questions is "no," but I'll try to make it a little longer. Second one first:

I don't think we ever used the word 'community.' We lived in a neighborhood that got larger as we grew older – at first, it was our street; then it stretched to our schools; and later, to the city. The contribution we made to our neighborhood was more about what we <u>didn't</u> do than what we did. We didn't litter; we didn't throw trash from cars or onto sidewalks; we didn't destroy or deface signs. We kept our yards clean and our grass cut.

We pretty much obeyed rules, and there were numerous grownups around to make sure of it. Play KICK THE CAN on the way home from school, and there was sure to be an adult on a porch to remind us to "pick that can up and dispose of it properly" when we got there!

Once my Girl Scout troop had a work party and tidied the garden of the church where we met. For once, we didn't have to wear the ugly green uniform. We could wear shorts and jerseys and tennis shoes, and we spent meeting time weeding and raking and sweeping. At our own church, my youth group delivered flyers about our Christmas Eve services and our Easter Sunrise worship, but this was mostly hanging something on a doorknob.

Neighborhoods were pretty self-sufficient then and didn't really want extra help. In emergencies, we called the fire department (only once that I remember in 18 years), and if someone got hurt while playing, Dr. Tamagna – a Russian lady physician who had a lovely accent - soothed our panics along with our cuts from her office in her home on the corner. Usually for free. There just seemed to be no need for grass roots action at that time.

Looking back, I realize that the activism taken for granted – even expected or required – now, is the result of the protests in the 1960's <u>for</u> Civil Rights and <u>against</u> the war in Viet Nam. Once people marched for change and it didn't come soon enough, they decided to change things themselves. I feel that the current ideas of 'giving back' and 'paying forward' and 'making a positive impact' came from those early protest movements.

However, by the time they took place, I was an adult with a husband and children, and those activities were for college kids. My generation felt that being a good citizen was important, and that meant abiding by rules already made, helping others when they needed it, voting, and writing to our congressmen if we were dissatisfied. It didn't involve in-your-face challenges like signs and marches. We DID like the folk songs about the grievances, however, and sang them hopefully.

Regarding voting – My first vote for a presidential candidate was for Barry Goldwater in 1964. At that time, you couldn't vote until you were 21, so I never got to vote for John F. Kennedy, which I would have done when he ran in 1960. I have to say that I really didn't know what he stood for, but he was young and handsome and had spoken at my high school graduation, so I was eager to see him become president. November 22, 1963 was a very sad day for me.

The amendment to vote when you turned 18 became a law in 1971 because of the protests mentioned above. Obviously, they accomplished some change!

As for performing, I really never took part in a major production – not even an amateur one.

Lack of opportunity was only slightly to blame. Although I was stage-struck at an early age, I demonstrated a singular lack of performing talent, mostly due to an undersupply of patience and resolve on my part. I was given piano lessons, but I found practice a bore, so after some years, I stopped going. I took acting classes too, but I remember only the exercises to increase projection of voice and lessons on how to cry on cue.

As for dance, ballet lessons for little girls were supposed to start early – at age six or so – and since I lived overseas from ages six to eight, no one thought it was possible to catch up when we finally settled back at home. If I had been really motivated, though, I probably could have proven them wrong, but I wasn't that excited about doing all those extra barre exercises. Instead, I took tap dancing, which was fun but also required daily practice. I wasn't willing to do that either and after an indifferent performance in a recital, I abandoned that idea too.

During elementary school years I took part in tableau-type school plays – churning butter in the pioneer skit, demonstrating duck and cover for the Safety Patrol presentation – and, at church, I was an alto angel in the Heavenly Host choir one Christmas Eve. I wore costumes for most of these appearances (or, in one case, a white choir robe), but I don't really consider them performances.

I have worked hard backstage, though, throughout most of my life. I worked on props and was in charge of drops and soft scenery for the Reading Civic Opera Society[3] for about ten years, and I even got to sing in the choruses of *Mame, Brigadoon,* and *Fiddler on the Roof* because the stage was big and needed people to fill it up. I got to wear costumes then, too!

Despite my inability to be someone else in front of others, I think teaching is a performance art and that an acting class should be required for all teacher trainees. I have used drama in my ESL classes since 1993 because it helps pronunciation and fluency. Every class lecture I give is a performance with audience participation, and the students' success on tests is the applause.

SO, I HAVE ACTUALLY BEEN 'PERFORMING' MY ENTIRE PROFESSIONAL LIFE, AND I HAVE ALWAYS FELT LIKE A STAR WITH A GREAT SUPPORTING CAST.

---

[3] Reading PA

What dolls and stuffed animals were important to you as a child?

I had two favorite dolls that I kept for a long time in case I had a little girl to give them to. Rose was a baby doll with a china head, and she had been my mother's. I kept her on my bed against the pillows when I wasn't playing dolls, and in a wagon when we went for walks. She always wore a nightgown or something that looked like a christening dress, and I had to be so careful of her that I didn't change her clothes very often. I didn't pretend with her very much either. I just took care of her.

Marianne was the fashion doll, and I dressed her up in something different every day. She had lots of clothes, thanks to Mom who made her new wardrobe items every time there was an occasion that called for presents. She had a suit for Sundays, and a warm coat for winter, and a long blue organdy dress for parties, among other outfits. In fact, she was better dressed than I was. She didn't tear things or get them dirty, though, so I suppose she deserved to have them.

When my friends and I played with dolls together, we mostly had tea parties or pretended to be in school with the dolls as pupils. When I was by myself, I also played school, but it was always a reading group – no arithmetic or other lessons! Marianne was the main student, but Rose sat in a chair and listened to the stories being read. And I figured out how to have more students in the class.

In 1947 or so, Hallmark made a series of cards featuring children from different countries of the world. Someone gave me one for my fourth birthday, and that began my collection. For several years, any occasion that called for a card brought another member of my personal United Nations.

The cards opened from the bottom and had a verse inside telling about the country the card child was from. The front of the card had the face and front body of the child, and the other half had the back. Each figure wore a typical costume from the country – like a kimono or an Eskimo tunic.

Because they could stand up, they were ideal 'students' for my school. Marianne sat in a chair on one side. The rest of the 'class' consisted of the card children which I lined up in front of Marianne. They each took turns 'reading' whatever book or lesson I had chosen for the afternoon, starting with Marianne and usually finishing with Rita from Brazil. Rose always sat next to me. I'm pretty sure my read-aloud ability stems from all the school I played before I was twelve.

I never slept with my dolls. Neither was soft, and Rose was fragile, so it wouldn't have been a good idea anyway. I don't remember a stuffed toy, either, but I did have a blanket with a satin edge which I called my pinky, and I slept with that until it almost disintegrated. I think we left the remnants in Japan!

The next part of this answer is <u>How Marianne Got Her Name.</u> My Grandma Hattie told me this story, and I decided to name Marianne after it.

HOW MARIANNE GOT HER NAME

Once there was a little girl who could <u>not</u> remember her times-tables, especially the 9-times-tables, and most especially 9 X 6. Every day she repeated the numbers as she walked to school, and each time she got stuck at "Nine times six is…"

This little girl had a doll that she loved very much and played with as often as she could. The doll's name was Marianne, and in the morning before school the little girl dressed her in a nice outfit, and at night she changed her into a nightgown and robe and put her to bed.

After school, girl and doll played together – sometimes outside, but most often in the bedroom having tea parties and playing school. The little girl loved school almost as much as she loved Marianne, so she repeated all the day's lessons by teaching them to her doll. Even so, remembering her multiplication tables was too difficult. Finally, she asked her grandmother for help.

"How," she begged, "can I remember nine times six?"

"Can you remember your doll's name?" her grandmother asked.

"Oh, yes," the little girl replied. "It's Marianne."

"Well, then, name your doll 54," said Grandma. "Each time you play with her call her 54. Then you'll remember what 9 X 6 is."

The little girl took her grandma's advice and renamed her dolly 54, and she didn't get stuck on 9 X 6 anymore because she thought of Marianne and remembered that she was now 54.

One day, the teacher gave an oral test on the times tables. The little girl felt confident that she could answer any question that came to her, so she sat up straight and waited happily for her turn. Sure enough, when she was called on, the teacher asked her, "How much is nine times six?"

The little girl smiled, took a deep breath, and said proudly,

"NINE TIMES SIX IS MARIANNE!"

Did you have any pets as a child? If not, did your friends have any that you took care of while they were gone or anything?

Mom was not fond of animals, so Corky was the only pet we had while I was a child. He came to us from the dog pound after we got home from Japan. He was the only dog on our street – in my memory, anyway. An enthusiastic playmate when we wanted to run, he would scamper along as we raced down the hill to the backyard fence or to the corner of Fulton and Taylor Streets. He was friendly and obedient, never running away or growling at people or other animals. I don't even think he chased squirrels!

During quiet times outdoors he stretched out on a porch step or sat wagging his tail and waiting to be invited into the game. Indoors, he curled up on the landing while we read or played games, and at dinner time, he sat respectfully in the doorway, alert to any sign that he might be offered a taste.

Our kitten, Flower, was acquired before we went to Japan. He was an outdoor pet that we fed sometimes, but he mostly caught mice and other rodents. He usually slept in a box on the back porch, or in the basement in cold weather. I don't know what arrangements we made for him when we left. Since he was pretty self-sufficient, probably none. He had become huge and looked more like the skunk he was named for than a cat. I don't recall his being a part of the family when we came back.

In Japan we had a pair of parakeets. One was green and one was blue. Bobby (your Papa) remembers them better than I do since he was home more than I was. In fact, he reminded me that we had them because I had forgotten, and my memory of them is still vague. I can't tell you their names or what happened to them, but I'm sure we found them good homes before we returned to the States.

None of my friends had pets that I recall. Mostly they came to our house to play with Corky. At least two of my friends' parents refused to get them any pet at all, but we were lucky that Dad was able to persuade Mom to let us have one. He had had a collie dog named Dickie, and he and Uncle Bill often reminisced about 'Dickie Dog' when they were together. I have a shadowy memory of a large hairy dog lying next to an old man's chair (probably my great- grandfather), but I don't know if this is a memory of seeing it for real or in a photograph. I am sending you a picture of your great-great grandmother Nixon and Dickie Dog, taken in about 1930.

I wrote a little story about Corky in the Slinky book. It mostly involves Beth, but there are some other things about him and how we got him. Take a look at it, and if you want to know more let me know - or ask your Papa.

NATALIE PEACOCK HARITOS (FORMERLY NIXON) AND DICKEY DOG

ADULT REFLECTIONS

Storyworth Questions

WHAT WAS YOUR FIRST BIG TRIP AS AN ADULT?

"Bucket list" was not a '60's phrase, but we had one anyway. Our version was labeled "What I have always wanted to do," and number one on that list was 'Take a trip to Europe.'

NOT 'Take a tour,' mind you! A 'trip' was different from a 'tour.'

As devout followers of Arthur Frommer and his <u>Europe on $5 a Day</u>, we scorned the "if it's Tuesday, it must be Belgium" travel treks that rushed you from place to place and counted lunch as a visit to a country. As members of this cult, we considered independent travel the only way to go, so we decided to do it ourselves and follow the rituals in his guidebook.

Like good Frommer believers we started planning and saving. First, we read every word of his book. As advised, we also read art books and history books and city guidebooks. Next, we began picking up brochures at travel shows and asking endless and envious questions of people who had 'been there.'

We collected and wrote down advice about museum exhibits and dress codes at churches and guided tours of palaces. We spent endless hours calculating distance and travel times between various cities, reluctantly discarding far-flung destinations like Spain and southern Italy that didn't fit into our limited time frame.

It was a good thing we were so occupied because it took us two years to accumulate both money and vacation days. We saved sick days and holidays. We worked extra hours. We figured out various schedules that included 3-day weekends – anything that would give us 21-plus days of travel. Above all, we saved money by eating lots of hamburger, rarely going to the movies, and vacationing with our parents when we needed a break. When I recall this time, I think about it as part of the trip even though we seldom left home.

In the autumn of 1965, we were finally ready. We were going to Europe for three whole weeks! We were to leave on September 3rd, the Friday before Labor Day, and return on September 27th. The plane ticket cost 25% of my annual salary, and Bob's hand trembled slightly as he signed the $1,000-dollar check. It was the largest amount of money we had ever spent at one time. And because our only credit card was for gas, we bought an additional $1,000 of travelers' checks to cash as needed. All that was left to do was pack. There was a chapter in The Book on that, too.

Even after all this preparation, the trip did not begin well!

The Book never said anything about flight problems. After a four-hour bus ride and short hops on a series of public transport vehicles, we arrived at JFK Airport to discover that our transatlantic flight had been overbooked.

Pan Am was apologetic and helpful and rebooked us on an Air France flight that left two hours later. In addition, they actually bought us a drink in a private lounge, just as if we were big spenders who might take our money elsewhere if inconvenienced.

Inconvenience, however, wasn't the problem: it was our schedule of sightseeing. We had carefully planned our three-and-a-half days in Paris by hours, and now we had two fewer than before. "What would we have to give up because of this?" we wondered anxiously.

Nothing, it turned out!

The plane was almost empty, so we had a full night's sleep, stretching out on an entire row of seats each. So much for the nap time we had scheduled. When we landed, an airline representative whisked us through customs and immigration and helped us change money. We felt like VIPs as we blew past the lines of our fellow passengers.

Another representative arranged our flight to Zurich on Thursday, booked our hotel (p. 148 in The Book), and got a car to take us to its door. Since this took about a half an hour, and since we were on our way before our flight's passengers had even claimed their luggage, our time plan was restored, and we didn't miss a thing.

After this initiation, the trip went as planned. We visited France, Switzerland, West Germany, Holland, England, and Ireland, averaging three and a half days in each – just about the same amount of time as on an escorted tour. BUT we controlled our schedule, and that was the objective for Arthur acolytes.

It has been over five decades since we took this trip, and we have lived abroad three times during those years – twice in Europe. Yet some of our first impressions have remained, no matter how many repeat visits we have made or other wonders we have seen.

We haven't forgotten the gaudy opulence of Versailles, especially since it was raining the day we visited, and the outside world provided a drab contrast to the flamboyant décor. The floodlit Notre Dame cathedral reflected in the Seine is a mind picture that stays with us still, as well as the eerie blue atmosphere in the ice cave beneath a glacier in the Swiss Alps.

In West Germany, a walk around the wall of Rothenberg actually took us <u>through</u> the cathedral – a Mighty Fortress, indeed! The recollection of climbing the stairs behind the bookcase in Anne Frank's House in Amsterdam is as poignant now as it was in 1965, and after seeing *Hamlet* performed in Shakespeare's birthplace, I promised myself that I would see all his plays live. This is a goal I am still trying to fulfill.

Also in Rothenburg, we conducted our first accommodation negotiation entirely *auf Deutsch*.

All by ourselves! Without looking up any words!

An elderly man approached us as we parked our rental car in the town square. "Mochten Sie ein Zimmer?" he asked. (Astutely, we knew he was asking a question because of the upward inflection - and - we knew that 'Zimmer' meant 'room.')

"Ich habe ein nett doppel Zimmer. Nur zehn mark." he continued. (We also knew our numbers. This was $5 a day territory!)

Nodding vigorously (a bi-lingual gesture) we said, "Ja." (How fluent.)

He gestured for us to follow him and led the way to the room, helpfully pointing out things to see and do as we walked along. At least, we assumed that was what he was doing. He said something about the 'kirche' and an 'Uhr' while pointing to a church and a clock.

The room was small, with no towels and no hot water, but the bed was comfortable and the location convenient, so we agreed to take it and settled into our first self-rented accommodation. We were very pleased with ourselves, and we like to think that Arthur and our respective German teachers would be proud.

On a personal and more embarrassing level, I still squirm when I remember getting sick in public after drinking mead at a medieval banquet in Bunratty Castle in Ireland, and I committed a number of faux pas while hosting high tea in the Dorchester Hotel in London.

I had invited a friend to this luxury hotel for this very English custom, and, as hostess, I was supposed to pour. Other groups were sitting in the lounge partaking also, and there was a low civilized murmur. I surreptitiously watched them to see how it was done and then grasped the silver teapot handle to pour a cup for my guest. My loud screech as my hand met the hot metal caused heads to swing around and then jerk back. It wasn't polite to stare, I guess. But I knew they were taking peeks occasionally as I struggled to tame the tea tray.

The spout of the teapot was curved in such a way that I had to hold the cup far away from it so that the trajectory of the liquid would hit the center; the sugar tongs wouldn't open, so I ended up flipping the cubes into the cups with it closed; and I forgot to put the cream in first – all no-no's in posh society. My British friends love it when I tell this story and ask me about it over and over.

When the plane took off from Ireland's Shannon Airport, I think we were both ready to get home. Our senses were so saturated, and our minds so crammed with images and information that they could hold no more. We wanted to be somewhere non-stimulating and sort out all our impressions.

Telling friends and family helped, but that method was limited. We soon found that "How was your trip?" was not an invitation for a travelogue, so we narrated our experience in bits and pieces – hopping around from country to country, activity to activity, depending on who was doing the asking. We finally organized our 35mm slides into a half-hour presentation and had parties for our church and work friends. If we served wine and hors d'oeuvres, we figured, they would come to eat and be obliged to stay and listen.

This helped us fix our itinerary and experiences into our minds where they were joined by later journeys and other memories. The Frommer travel method is still our preferred one, although we have taken a few cruises and escorted excursions as we got older. But we travel independently when we can – TRIPS, not tours!

OUR FIRST BIG TRIP WAS JUST THE BEGINNING!

HOW IS LIFE DIFFERENT TODAY COMPARED TO WHEN YOU WERE A CHILD?

(Whew! What a question!)

No child today would recognize the world I grew up in. Heck, I don't even recognize it myself when I think back.

It was leisurely, I remember, and quiet. There was time for friends and time to be alone – which was okay, not a symptom of mental distress. It was safe to walk home from a friend's house at night. It was cheap to buy an ice cream cone. I remember when a scoop cost 5 cents, and my disappointment and chagrin when the price was raised to 8 cents – and I had only brought a nickel.

Our group games were spontaneously organized: hide and seek, baseball, jump rope, bike racing, sledding. We usually didn't have all the right equipment or proper protective gear. Our play spaces were unsafe by today's standards--streets, backyards, hard surfaces. No mediating adults were around to settle arguments. Yet, I don't recall any major injuries (unless you count skinned knees or cut fingers), or any lasting relationship breaks.

Communication was mostly in person because houses had only one telephone, and we kids weren't encouraged to "tie up the line" unless it was necessary. Our family had a single line just for us, but my grandmother still had a party line. If you picked up the receiver in her house and heard someone talking, you were supposed to hang up and wait until they were finished. Sometimes we listened until Grandma caught us. We were scolded for 'eavesdropping' (a word we didn't know, and which sounded AWFUL), and we were not allowed to touch the phone for the rest of the day.

Without an answering machine (these weren't available until the mid-80's), calls were often missed. If you weren't home, or someone was talking on your phone, the caller would get long, hollow rings or the angry buzz of a busy signal until he hung up. Unless he tried again, you might never know about the attempted contact.

On the bright side, however, it was much easier to dodge someone you didn't want to talk to. "Gosh, I'm sorry. I wasn't home when you called. I've already promised (_fill in the blank_) I'd go with him" was a gentle way of refusing an undesirable date.

Television was in its childhood too. At first, programming was scheduled for the evenings – from approximately 5 to 10 PM, depending on where you lived. It gradually expanded. At first it came to the earlier parts of the day and then to later at night. Even so, the channel always signed off and displayed the station's test pattern by 11:30 at the latest. CNN's 24-hour news did not begin until 1980.

Generally, moms were at home when the children were. If, for some very good reason like a family business or maybe survival, a mother had to work, a grandmother, an aunt, or an older child was in charge. No child I knew was what was later called a latchkey kid.

Public school was pretty similar throughout the country, especially elementary school: alphabet and printing in kindergarten; reading, numbers and counting in 1st grade; the beginnings of cursive writing and basic math in 2nd grade; and so forth. If you went to a private school – usually church affiliated – it was the same except that you wore a uniform and learned about the Bible also.

We didn't read the Bible in our public-school classes, but each morning, before we began lessons, we recited the Pledge of Allegiance, including 'one nation under God' (I always capitalized God in my mind, but others might not have), and we also prayed The Lord's Prayer – until 1954 when the 'no prayer in schools' movement surfaced. Ironically, 1954 was when 'under God' officially became part of the Pledge and tripped us up until we remembered to include it. God was both out and in - go figure!

Bad behavior was punished by reduction of privileges like not getting to feed the class pet or not leading the lunch line. There were a few fights on the playground – nothing violent – which were easily broken up. Sometimes there was what they now call 'bullying' or 'shaming' that made us cry a little. Being called "fatty" by a group of jeering boys or being ignored by the "best" girls devastated us for a day or so, but if I polled my contemporaries, I doubt if I would find any lasting trauma because of the early ridicule.

I sometimes call my childhood "adulthood training," We were all learning to be grownups.

I remember learning the proper way to wash dishes (no dishwashing machines anywhere). Glasses first, then silverware, then china, then pots and pans. One of us (my brother or I) washed, the other dried. Mom supervised. I learned to iron, starting with Dad's handkerchiefs, and progressing to pillowcases and skirts. Some things had to be sprinkled (I got my first steam iron as a wedding gift), so I was in high school before I was allowed to iron Dad's white shirts. I learned to respect the stove when I popped corn and made fudge.

I felt very prepared when I left home.

Now it seems as if our children are training us! Our grandchildren are guiding us through computer settings and app downloads on our smartphones. They are teaching us how to text, and 'share' on Facebook. They are correcting our vocabulary (policeman/police officer) and our pronouns ('they' rather than 'he' or 'she'); they encourage us to wear slacks and flipflops to church (designer ones, of course).

The present generation is better educated and more accomplished than we were; their talents, athletic ability, and technical knowledge are being developed to an unprecedented degree. But I wonder—

Do kids ever play in each other's backyards without a play date? When they go home after school, is anyone there? Do they talk to each other or just text?

I GUESS I JUST DON'T UNDERSTAND 21ST CENTURY CHILDHOOD.

WHAT SMALL DECISION YOU MADE HAD A BIG IMPACT ON YOUR LIFE?

It wasn't so much a small decision as a quick one. One afternoon my husband, Bob, called me at work wanting to know if I were willing to go to South Korea for two years. I took about three minutes to think it over and said 'yes.'

We **had** talked about it previously – a little – when we heard the rumor that his firm had a job there. It was a "wouldn't it be fun to...." sort of conversation, and neither of us thought any more about it. But here he was on the phone saying, "Korea's heating up again. Are you still willing to go?"

My co-workers were dumbfounded that I could make a decision in less than five minutes that would disrupt our lives so completely. They were even more shocked when they realized that the move was taking place in the next two months.

It was a scramble. We needed to decide what to take (????? pound limit on what we could ship); we had to find storage for the things left behind; we had to rent our house; and both our boys had been hit by a car that spring. While Bobby had recovered, Bryan was still in a body cast because of a broken femur.

This complicated things like passport photos, visa applications, and doctor clearances. We had to have physicals and shots. We had to get school records. We had to sign papers. We had to set up bank accounts. We had to tell our families.

My family were happy for us. They had taken Brother Bob and me and to Japan after the war, and there had been no ill effects from those two years: no trauma; no disease; no education gaps. So, they were encouraging and excited. Hubby Bob's family were uncertain, however. No one from the Brems side had a yen to travel and didn't really understand why we would want to go "so far away."

We solved most of the problems easily. Surprisingly, once Bryan was out of the cast, his doctor gave his blessing, only stipulating that we get regular X-rays while we were gone; the firm helped with storage and paperwork; my brother and his wife would use and look after our car; Brems relatives were comforted that we were to be nowhere near the DMZ.

The real problem became the house rental. We advertised for several weeks but had no takers until a group of people who wanted to try Christian communal living as described in the Biblical book of Acts, came to look at it. This motley assortment of folks looked it over, enthusing especially about the seven bedrooms. Then, they came down to the living room, lit a candle and held a prayer meeting that included rocking back and forth and speaking in a sort of babble, while Bobby, Bryan and I looked on.

God must have approved because no one else called.

By mid-July we departed, spending time with family and friends as we crossed the US. We flew to Hawaii, Okinawa, and Japan en route to Seoul. We even had a refueling stop in Guam. In Korea, we took the train to Pusan at the tip of the peninsula on the Sea of Japan and were driven along the coast to the nuclear plant construction site which was where the job was. We were to live on a temporary housing compound, built for foreign workers.

There we entered, not Korea, but Great Britain! And this became the source of the biggest impact.

The project was a joint British/American one, so there was just a handful of engineers from the United States at the site. They were mostly managers – older couples with no children. Nice, but not particularly social. Our sons, ages 9 and 6, found their companions among the British youngsters who welcomed them into the circle. In a week they had acquired at least ten new friends and a variety of British accents.

We soon followed suit. Our adult social life also became English. We discovered that they didn't just drink tea!

Darts and pints at the bar; potlucks at private houses; bridge, and cutthroat badminton games, and dances at the clubhouse. We entered in enthusiastically. Foreign became familiar. In two years, we made contacts that have lasted for nearly five decades. I met my two best friends on that compound.

We didn't neglect Korea either. The American expats were not adventurous, but the Brits explored all the options outside the fence. We tagged along when a group went to a local, makeshift restaurant, and ate kimchi and bulgogi that none of the US families would touch. We took language lessons from a native teacher.

The site asked me to teach an English class, and through my engineer students we took excursions to ancient temples and city landmarks. We contacted some missionaries and helped ease a Korean pastor's study trip to the United States. Through an international women's group, I helped support an orphanage and had the opportunity to escort some adopted children to their new homes in Europe.

When we left two years later, we continued our trip westward and completed a trip around the world, something Bryan told his 4th grade class when we got home. His teacher didn't believe him. We stopped in Thailand, India, Sri Lanka, Indonesia, West Germany and England before landing in New York. We even set foot in Iran – two years before the hostage situation made that country too dangerous to visit.

This experience didn't just change our lives for two years. It changed them forever. After the first rush of euphoria at being home again, we all itched to continue traveling. In less than two years, we again took a foreign assignment.

We developed enduring empathy for minorities, having been noticeably foreign whenever we ventured off the compound. We gained confidence in our abilities to adapt to unfamiliar language and food and surroundings. We now understand the difficulties foreigners in our country face as they struggle with a strange culture and language.

We also came to cherish our own country's blessings of bounty. And freedom. And advantage. No matter where we roamed, we were always grateful to it for welcoming us back.

No other decision we made had such a profound effect on us.

THE WORLD IS A NEIGHBORHOOD NOW.

ACKNOWLEDGEMENTS

I need to thank a number of people for this work in progress.

My first thanks should go to my brother, Cleon Robert Nixon III (Bobby), who – sixty years or so ago – had the idea for this book. Throughout this time, he kept these stories alive whenever two or three family members gathered. I am glad that we reminisced so often and kept the memories close.

I appreciate my sister-in-law, Judy Vician Nixon, and my sister, Beth Nixon Sheets, for their interest in this project. Their memories filled in my lapses thereof, and their suggestions for topics filled a number of pages. Their ideas and corrections were invaluable and made my writing much clearer and better.

I must thank my parents, too. They created the home atmosphere that I tried to capture in these stories and gave me and my siblings the experiences, the guidance, and the love that made my childhood so much fun.

Several friends read bits and pieces of this and encouraged me to continue. I am grateful to Frances Octon in England, Peggy Chadwick Niblack in Myrtle Beach, and Vedran Mutic in Luxembourg for the positive feedback on several of the anecdotes. My husband, Bob Brems, deserves thanks for listening to my recollections and for giving me time and space to write them.

My grandson, John Brems, deserves a big thank you for guiding me through the computer intricacies of this project. His patient explanations soothed my frustration with technology and enabled me to get the manuscript into shape.

I am also grateful to Olivia Szczawinski for creating the cover, especially because she drew exactly what I wanted, even though I couldn't explain it.

And finally, the COVID-19 pandemic had a lot to do with this book being written, so I would like to acknowledge its contribution. The necessity to shelter in place for so long is responsible for my finally buckling down and putting my memories into words.

The cover design is by Olivia Szczawinski who is a wife and a mother of two, with a BFA from Kutztown University in Pennsylvania. She enjoys diving into creative outlets whenever they present themselves. This has led to painting wedding cakes, crafting cake toppers, running children's art programs, and even designing book covers.

Illustrations are mostly family photos.

Picture credit: https://yohidevils.net/misc/ships/cgmorton.htm

Any others are from istockphoto.com.

AFTERWORD

O nce upon a time, my brother and I planned to write a book about our family. We just wanted to record some of our day-to-day experiences so we wouldn't forget them.

For several reasons – other stories – this collaboration never happened, and now I find myself alone with memories which will disappear unless I put them down and pass them on.

Our family was not remarkable or famous or even especially talented; we were just remarkably ordinary. There were so many memoirs about heroes, and missionary families, and famous families, and even dysfunctional families, that Bobby and I felt there needed to be an account about an everyday/ average brood.

Our family had a normal number of members – one father and one mother, two daughters and a son. There were two grandmothers, one who lived close and one who came on extended visits and made bread; we had an average number of aunts, uncles and cousins and a few aunts-and-uncles-by-courtesy that were close friends and godparents. There was also a step-grandpa who only had one arm, and Grandpa Nixon who lived in faraway Oklahoma and whom we never saw.

We lived in a small, red-brick colonial house in the calm suburbs of an exciting city, but the excitement didn't really reach us. We had an almost-Schnauzer named Corky, and a black and white kitten which we named Flower after Bambi's friend in the movie. Flower grew to be enormous and very unlike a flower, but he was so cute when he was little!

Dad worked for the Air Force at the Pentagon, but he always maintained that his job was making sure that the budget balanced and that US batteries fit into British radios. No excitement there!

Because the sitting president was the Commander in Chief at Dad's office, we were curiously non-political in a highly political area. We were respectful of our government leaders, and from habit, for most authority. I don't recall any jokes made at the expense of another person or group – either lofty or low. We seldom had a lasting personal controversy or argument.

So, where was the conflict? Every plot needs conflict, right? Why did we think we had a story to tell?

Because we had so much fun together. Because other people liked to come to our house rather than someone else's. Because, later on, when we talked about what we used to do, people looked at us incredulously – as if we had lived a fantasy life: kids sitting around a dinner table, talking to their parents? a family reading aloud in the evening instead of watching television? siblings who didn't fight with each other? To some, this stuff seemed story-bookish - unreal.

Most of all, though, our growing up years are part of a now-caricatured time, and our generation (The Silent Generation) is dismissed as insensitive and unaware of cultural divisions, ignorant of technology, old-fashioned, and incapable of adapting to 'better times'. We wanted people to know that the Fifties were not all bad, nor were we heedless. We and the decade were refreshingly alive, optimistic, and innocent of malice.

So, we decided to document our ordinary life in the hope readers will believe that there used to be a simpler way to live and, maybe, find it again. The 1950's were OUR golden age.

Made in the USA
Middletown, DE
18 April 2022